PHILIPS RESEARCH

100 years of inventions that matter

Dirk van Delft & Ad Maas

PHILIPS RESEARCH

100 years of inventions that matter

WBOOKS
Museum Boerhaave

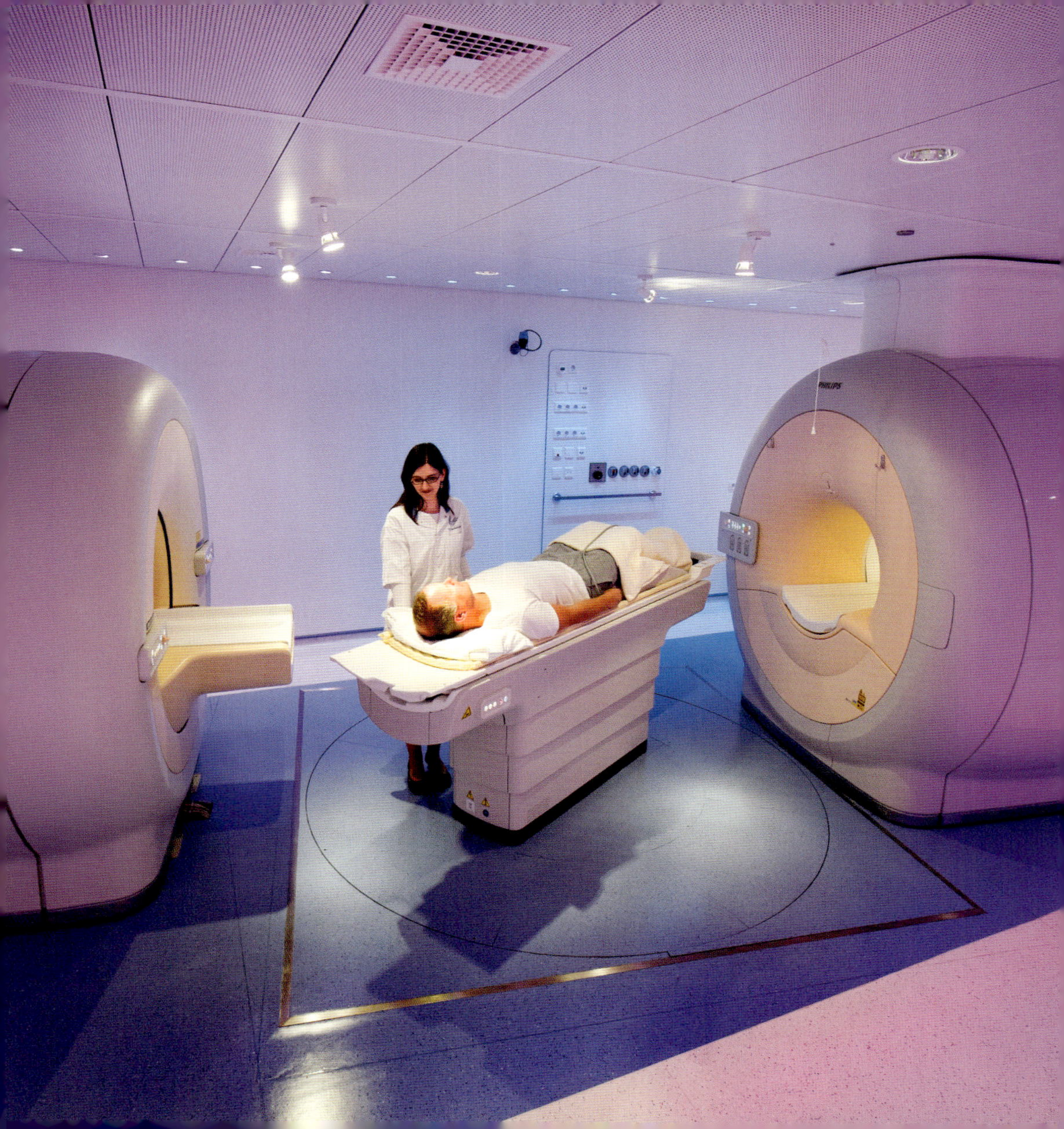
PHILIPS

Contents

Foreword

Philips is a part of the Dutch identity. The company that is lovingly known as the 'famous light-bulb factory in the South' is responsible for inventions that are a source of pride. From X-ray tubes for examining patients to street lighting with sodium lamps, and even to radio tubes. From the electric shaver with a rotating head to the cassette recorder and the Plumbicon tube for television cameras. From the rechargeable battery to the compact disc, and all the way to high-resolution MRI scanners. Recent inventions include the Airfloss, the RéAurora laser lamp for fighting the effects of skin ageing, and innovations in the area of lighting, including the 'luminous carpet', LED lamps with WiFi, and modulated light that can activate a tablet or smartphone.

These inventions have been developed at Philips Research, a company that now operates globally, with research laboratories in Bangalore, Briarcliff, Cambridge, Eindhoven (headquarters), Hamburg and Shanghai – with a location in Brazil under development. It all began on 2 January 1914, as the Philips Natuurkundig Laboratorium (Physics Laboratory) in Eindhoven – the renowned NatLab – with Gilles Holst as the first director. This book has been compiled to commemorate the centennial of Philips Research. The authors are affiliated with the Museum Boerhaave, which will be displaying the exhibition '100 YEARS OF INVENTIONS, Made by Philips Research' from 19 December 2013 through 26 October 2014.

Philips Research: 100 years of inventions that matter is intended primarily as a portrait of Philips Research, its renowned history and the people who have made the laboratory great. It also highlights the iconic products that have transformed Philips into a global brand. As demonstrated by the overview, 'inventions that matter' are not developed exclusively in laboratories. It is nearly impossible to say whether the success of the compact disc was largely a feat of research or whether it was a fine piece of marketing. Both aspects were indispensible. Without commercial instincts, gifted designers and refined marketing, Philips would never have become a giant in household items. Instead of trying to unravel all of these knots, we will present a colourful parade of objects brought forth by a century of Eindhoven creativity.

The cooperative assistance of the Philips Company Archives and the Stichting tot Behoud Historische Philipsproducten (Foundation for the Preservation of Historical Philips Products) was essential to the production of this book. We are extremely grateful to Jan Paulussen, Frans Vos and Mannie van Bruggen. Ferrie Aalders and Bert Spierings provided generous support within Philips Research.

The character of Philips Research has changed markedly throughout the past century. For a long time, the NatLab enjoyed an independent position, in which its researchers were allowed the freedom to do what they thought best, based on a firm belief that fundamental research would always yield applications. The research has since been synchronised to the direct wishes of the various operating sectors. Now that health and well-being have taken centre stage at Philips, the mission of Philips Research has been adjusted.
The central focus is now on improving the quality of human life through innovations that matter – innovations that lead to a sustainable, healthier world, made possible by new technologies.

The incandescent light bulb has been phased-out by Europe, and the headquarters of Philips have been relocated to Amsterdam. One aspect that has remained unchanged, however, is the effort to achieve 'game-changing innovations' that Philips can bring to the market. This would be impossible without a vital Philips Research.

Dirk van Delft
Director of Museum Boerhaave

Chemical laboratory, 1916.

The beginnings of Philips (1891-1914)

The electrification of public life, which emerged with the advent of the first commercial electric motors and generators around 1880, had far-reaching effects on society. Innovative companies seized the opportunity. Before long, the first telephones had found their way into the business world, and electric lighting began to replace the gas lamp and the oil lamp. Early producers of incandescent light bulbs included the American Edison Electric Light Company, the British Swan Electric Light Company Ltd. and the German AEG (Allgemeine Elektricitäts-Gesellschaft or General Electricity Company). In 1889, the Netherlands had four light-bulb factories, all of which were operating on the foreign market as well, in order to generate sufficient income. Two years later, Philips would join their ranks – and quickly overshadow them.

Philips & Co. was established on 15 May 1891 by Gerard Philips, with financial support from his prescient father, Frederik. The Philips family has its roots in Zaltbommel. Father Philips, a first cousin of Karl Marx, was a banker and traded in coffee and tobacco. As the eldest son, Gerard (1858) attended the Hogere Burgerschool in Arnhem at the same time that Hendrik Antoon Lorentz was teaching mathematics there. In 1876, he matriculated at the Poly-technical School in Delft (now known as TU Delft) as a student of civil engineering and architecture, graduating seven years later as a mechanical engineer.

Gerard was a hard-working technician with a hunger for enterprise. After completing his studies, he began a career in the shipbuilding industry, first at De Schelde in Vlissingen and, in 1885, at a wharf in Glasgow. He was fascinated by the installation of electric lighting in ships, which was then in full swing. He followed an educational programme in 'Electric lighting and transmission of power' at the University of Glasgow and was offered a position in the 1886-1887 Research Group of the Natural Philosophy Department, under the supervision of the future Lord Kelvin.

In his examinations, Gerard won the silver medal for scoring the highest number of points. He had found his calling. In 1887, Gerard Philips took a position at the Anglo-American Brush Electric Light Corporation in London, which was one of the largest electric lighting companies at that time. He soon made plans with the company to establish a light-bulb factory in the Netherlands, but the English partners eventually withdrew. This was merely a delay. After becoming a representative for AEG in Berlin in 1890, Gerard started his Dutch light-bulb factory anyway. In short, Gerard Philips knew what he was doing in 1891, when he began producing incandescent light bulbs in a vacant factory on Emmasingel in Eindhoven – which is now the location of the Philips Museum.

Gerard had selected Eindhoven for its inexpensive labour, good rail connections and trained personnel – owing to the cigar industry. He knew his way around the world of industry, understood the importance of patents, had acquired the necessary professional knowledge (e.g. for manufacturing carbon filaments) and had made close observations during a tour of Dutch light-bulb producers. He immersed himself in ordering machines, dynamos, measuring equipment, chemicals and semi-manufactured goods (e.g. lamp caps and glass bulbs).

One remarkable characteristic of the young Philips was his focus on a single product: the carbon-filament lamp. The company took on the competition with smaller and larger companies, for which light bulbs were part of a larger range of products. The factory on Emmasingel was initially started on a small scale, in order to gain experience. Business was good, despite occasional problems related to the development of proper manuals, the introduction of standardisation and the manufacture of precision instruments during the preparatory phase. When Philips began to turn a profit in 1894, the factory space was expanded. During the 1895-1905 period, production increased by a factor of twenty, ultimately reaching four million light bulbs. Philips & Co. expanded to become the third-largest producer of light bulbs in Europe, following AEG and Siemens & Halske.

This success was largely due to the arrival of Anton Philips in the company. More than 15 years younger than his brother Gerard, Anton had not been particularly successful at school. Upon his arrival in Eindhoven, however, the friendly and generous 20-year-old proved to have been born to sell. In 1899, Anton became a partner in the firm, with Gerard as the general and technical director. Their father, Frederik, died in 1900. The brothers complemented each other quite well. While Anton preferred to devote his efforts to sales, Gerard combined the tasks of a manufacturer/entrepreneur with those of a director and a builder.
He continued his intensive involvement with the quality of manufacturing processes, even after several years, when the Philips organisation had undergone major expansion.

The working relationship between Anton and Gerard more than resolved the classic rivalry between technology and commerce, which tends to pose an obstacle for many companies. Moreover, their interaction was an asset to the company,

Gerard Philips conducting his first experiments attempting to use cellulose for the manufacture of carbon filaments, 1890.

Anton Philips in 1911.

and it became one of the pillars in the success of Philips. The combination of a solid organisation, sound financial management and an open attitude towards technological innovation with Anton's capacity for hard negotiations formed the foundation for an exceptionally strong competitive position. Philips became a dominant player within the turbulent global market for light bulbs, alongside the American General Electric and such European companies as Siemens & Halske and the Compagnie Générale d'Electricité. In order to neutralise the competition, the European producers of carbon-filament lamps formed a cartel in 1903: Verkaufsstelle Vereinigter Glühlampenfabriken (VVG).

Staff of Philips & Co, 1891.

On 9 October 1907, the Philips' Metaalgloeilampen-fabriek (Philips Metal Filament Lamp Factory) was established in Eindhoven. The manufacture of metal filament lamps (e.g. using osmium and tantalum) was incorporated into this separate company, which was soon producing up to 20,000 units per day. Because lamps with metal filaments burned at much higher temperatures than carbon lamps, they produced more light.

To make these filaments, Philips opened its own chemical laboratory in 1909. The company quickly developed into a modern industry, based on mass production. Meanwhile, the production of carbon filament lamps in Eindhoven had been declining. In 1912, all of the activities were combined into a single corporation: the Philips' Gloeilampenfabrieken (Philips Incandescent Lamp Company). Gerard and Anton Philips were both directors.

Gerard stepped down 10 years later and transferred the entire directorate to his brother Anton.
At that time (1 April 1922), Philips had around 5.500 employees. The company had just started expanding into foreign markets and the production of radio tubes. Gerard Philips remained affiliated with the company as a commissioner until 1939. In the same year, Anton – under whose leadership Philips had developed into a multi-national in the 1930s – stepped down as chairman of the board. His son-in-law, Frans Otten, accepted the torch, which he would pass on to Anton's son Frits in 1961. Gerard had no children.

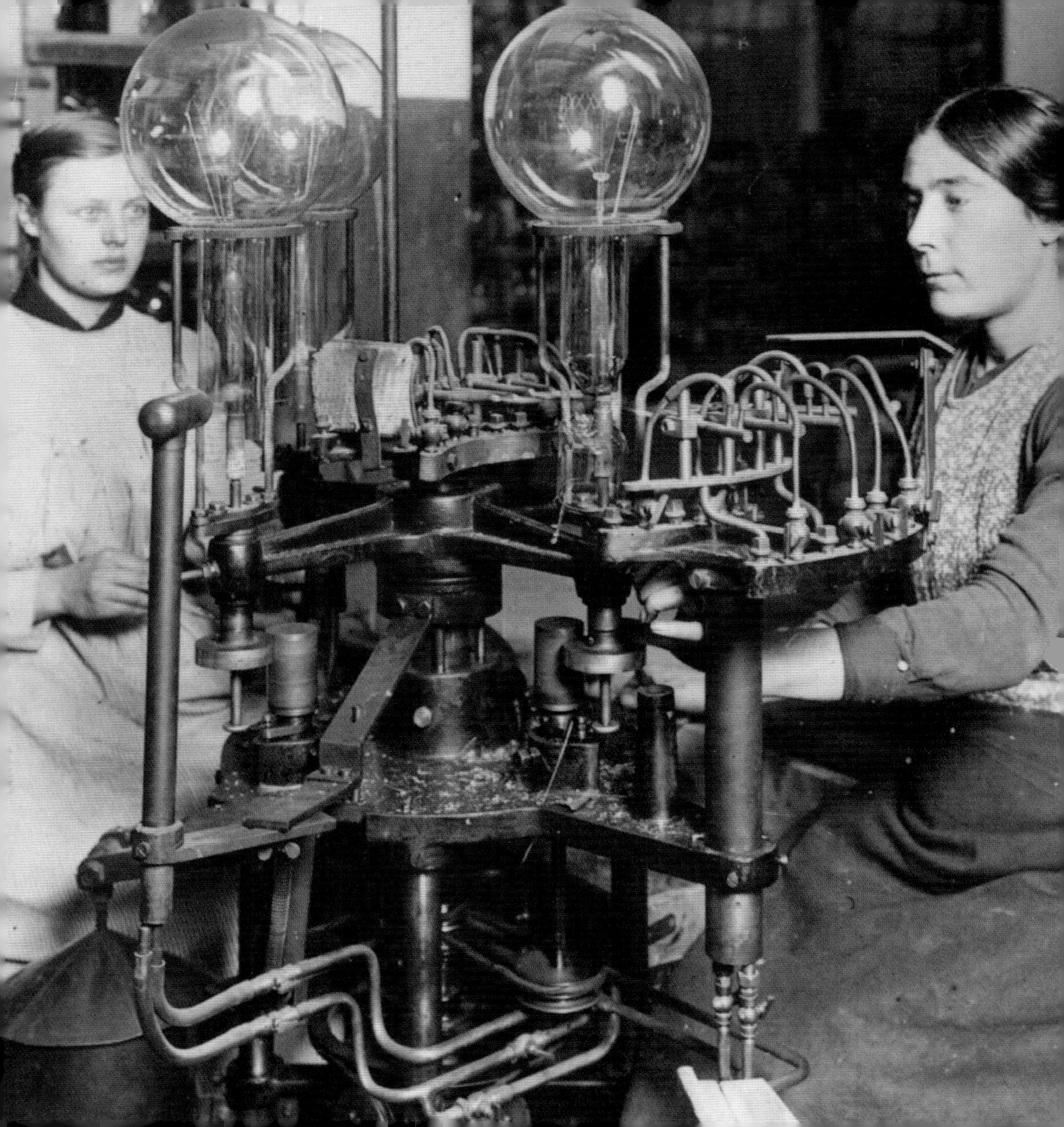

1. Industrial heritage

Philips began his activities in 1891, in a small vacant factory on Vrijstraat (later, Emmasingel), in the heart of Eindhoven. Business went well, and a new, much larger factory was opened across the street in 1897. From this home base, the Philips empire continued to expand. In the 1920s, factories, laboratories and offices sprang up like mushrooms. Many locations have since been closed for various reasons (e.g. obsolescence, pressure to reduce costs, changes in the strategic course). In many cases, these locations were housed in remarkable buildings.

What should be done with this industrial architectural heritage? In Eindhoven, the Lichttoren (Light Tower), the Witte Dame (White Lady), the Klokgebouw (Clock Building) and the Evoluon have been designated as monuments. In Strijp, where the rapidly expanding Philips company built factories and laboratories in the 1920s, the Natuurkundig Laboratorium (NatLab), the Veemgebouw and the Hoge Rug (High Ridge; originally four attached factories for assembling radios and television sets) have been saved from demolition. They have acquired new functions within a new urban community that offers considerable space to creativity and design. The Witte Dame, a former factory on the Emmasingel reflecting the New Objectivity of the 1930s, currently houses the Design Academy Eindhoven and the library.

Philips continues to be associated with Eindhoven. Nevertheless, the headquarters was relocated to the Rembrandt Tower in Amsterdam in 1998, under the direction of Cor Boonstra. Since 2001, it has been located in the Breitner Tower, close to the Amstel railway station.

The immaterial heritage of Philips is displayed in the building at 24 Looyenbeemd, a treasury on the outskirts of Eindhoven. It is managed by the volunteers of the Stichting tot Behoud van Historische Philips Producten (Foundation for the Preservation of Historic Philips Products).

The first Philips factory

The small factory on Emmasingel was originally constructed as a nail factory, and it was later used to produce buckskin and sheets. In 1891, Frederik and Gerard Philips bought the building for 12,150 Dutch guilders and manufactured carbon filament lamps there under the name of Philips & Co. When a larger factory was completed on the other side of the street, 31 Emmasingel was used as a chemical storage facility and a warehouse. Later, fluorescent powder for fluorescent lamps was produced there. From 1951 through 1991, the building served as a demonstration laboratory for Philips Lighting, after which it became the home of the Philips archives. On 5 April 2013, following a thorough renovation, Queen Beatrix re-opened the national monument as the Philips Museum.

In front of the new factory

This group photograph of the Philips staff dates from 1916. It was taken in front of the new factory on Emmasingel, which was opened in 1897.

The symbol of Philips

The Lichttoren (Light Tower), which was once the headquarters of the Philips Lighting division in Eindhoven, dates from 1921. Rising above the former light-bulb factory, this seven-sided building was designed by Dirk Roosenburg. The building was used for testing lamps, hence the name. Philips sold this remarkable building in 1999.

The complex currently houses a grand café, a hotel, apartments and businesses.

The forbidden city

In the early 1920s, Philips established a location in the Strijp district in Eindhoven. Because the 27-hectare site was not freely accessible and surrounded by buildings, Strijp S was nicknamed 'the forbidden city'. The glass factory became the first tenant in 1916. The NatLab was located there six years later.

The Klokgebouw

Constructed in 1929 and with the striking Philips emblem on the roof, the Klokgebouw (Clock Building) was used for producing Bakelite. Because Bakelite was a registered trademark, however, the Philips version of the plastic was known as 'Philite'.

The Hoge Rug

The Hoge Rug (High Ridge), which consists of four connected factory buildings, was used largely for the production of radio and television sets. The Veemgebouw was also part of this complex.

Calisthenics at the company school

In 1929, Philips opened its own company school on Frederiklaan, between Philipsdorp and Strijp S. A dormitory located next to the school offered housing for students who lived far away. This Jongens Nijverheids Onderwijs (Boys' Industrial Education) was open to any boy who had completed primary school. Any student who completed the four-year programme successfully was guaranteed a job with Philips. The school also emphasised sound minds in sound bodies. Each day, the students had 15 minutes of outdoor calisthenics.

The flying saucer: Evoluon

In 1966, Philips opened the Evoluon, a flying saucer on stilts, with a diameter of 77 metres. It was designed by Louis Kalff and Leo de Bever. A gift commemorating Philips's 75th anniversary, the Evoluon proclaimed technological progress. Visitors flocked to the building, where they had the opportunity to fiddle with knobs themselves. Interest eventually declined as other hands-on exhibits opened elsewhere (e.g. the NINT in Amsterdam). Philips discontinued these activities in 1989 and transformed the Evoluon into an event and conference centre. In the summer of 2012 and 2013, the old Evoluon made a return appearance with a summer exhibition about the brain.

The NatLab at Complex W

In the 1960s, a new NatLab was constructed in Waalre, an independent municipality due south of Eindhoven. Anyone wishing to enter the site (which is now part of Eindhoven) had to pass a porter and a boom gate.

Since 2003, 'Complex W' has also provided room to other parties. Its name was changed to High Tech Campus Eindhoven, and the sign bearing the name 'Philips Research' was removed.

The Strip at the High Tech Campus

The High Tech Campus Eindhoven is freely accessible, in that the porters and barriers have been moved to the individual buildings. The HTC currently accommodates more than 100 companies and institutes, including about 40 start-ups. The prevailing philosophy is that of 'open innovation'. 'The Strip', a 400-metre-long building located on the water, houses a conference centre with an auditorium, various restaurants, shops and a Campus Wellness Center.

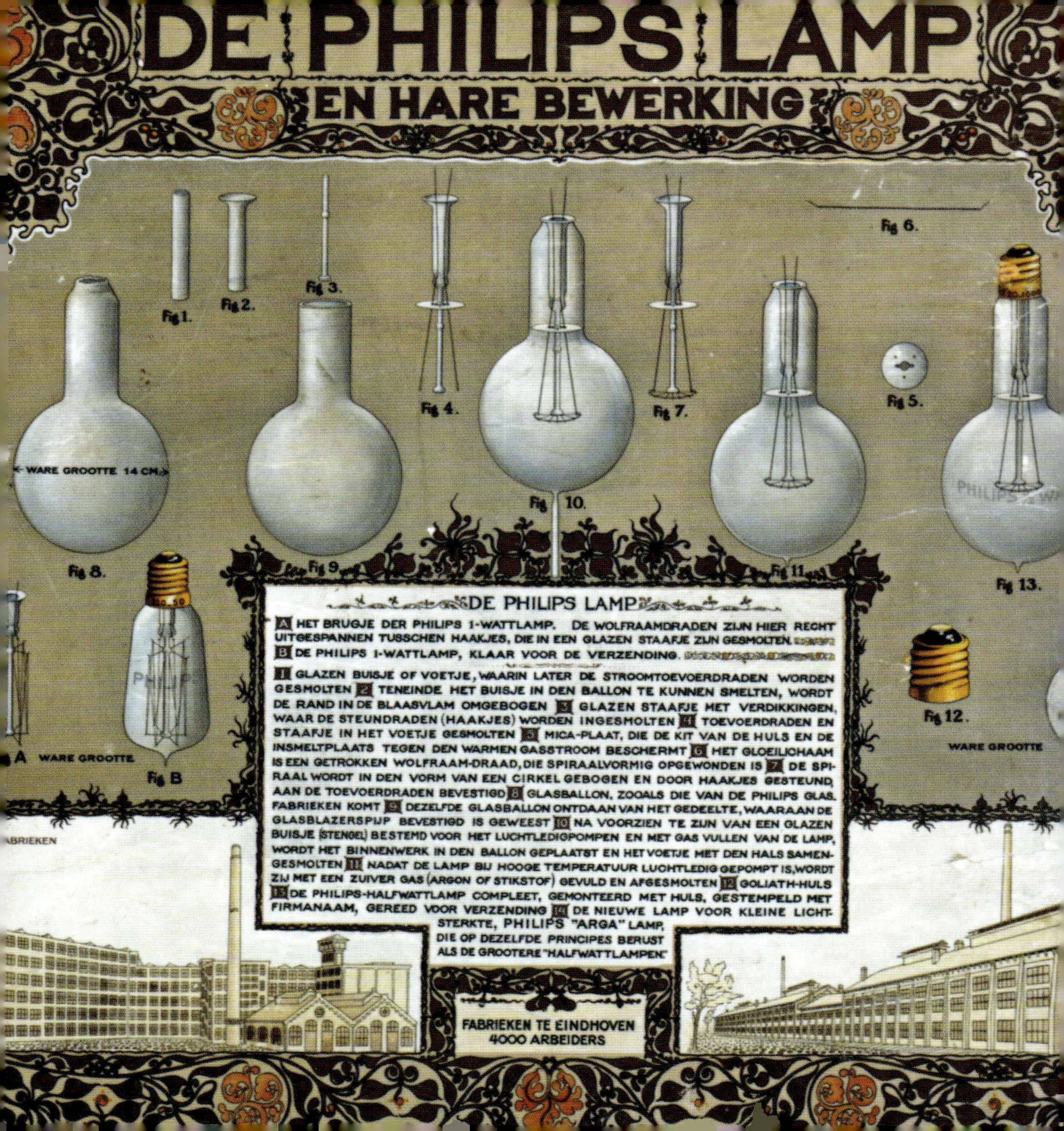
DE PHILIPS LAMP
EN HARE BEWERKING
Fig 1.
Fig 2.
Fig 3.
Fig 4.
Fig 10.
Fig 7.
Fig 6.
Fig 5.
Fig 8.
WARE GROOTTE 14 CM.
Fig 9
Fig 11
PHILIPS
Fig 13.
PHILIPS
A WARE GROOTTE
Fig B
Fig 12.
WARE GROOTTE
DE PHILIPS LAMP
A HET BRUGJE DER PHILIPS 1-WATTLAMP. DE WOLFRAAMDRADEN ZIJN HIER RECHT UITGESPANNEN TUSSCHEN HAAKJES, DIE IN EEN GLAZEN STAAFJE ZIJN GESMOLTEN.
B DE PHILIPS 1-WATTLAMP, KLAAR VOOR DE VERZENDING.
1 GLAZEN BUISJE OF VOETJE, WAARIN LATER DE STROOMTOEVOERDRADEN WORDEN GESMOLTEN 2 TENEINDE HET BUISJE IN DEN BALLON TE KUNNEN SMELTEN, WORDT DE RAND IN DE BLAASVLAM OMGEBOGEN 3 GLAZEN STAAFJE MET VERDIKKINGEN, WAAR DE STEUNDRADEN (HAAKJES) WORDEN INGESMOLTEN 4 TOEVOERDRADEN EN STAAFJE IN HET VOETJE GESMOLTEN 5 MICA-PLAAT, DIE DE KIT VAN DE HULS EN DE INSMELTPLAATS TEGEN DEN WARMEN GASSTROOM BESCHERMT 6 HET GLOEILICHAAM IS EEN GETROKKEN WOLFRAAM-DRAAD, DIE SPIRAALVORMIG OPGEWONDEN IS 7 DE SPIRAAL WORDT IN DEN VORM VAN EEN CIRKEL GEBOGEN EN DOOR HAAKJES GESTEUND, AAN DE TOEVOERDRADEN BEVESTIGD 8 GLASBALLON, ZOOALS DIE VAN DE PHILIPS GLASFABRIEKEN KOMT 9 DEZELFDE GLASBALLON ONTDAAN VAN HET GEDEELTE, WAARAAN DE GLASBLAZERSPIJP BEVESTIGD IS GEWEEST 10 NA VOORZIEN TE ZIJN VAN EEN GLAZEN BUISJE (STENGEL) BESTEMD VOOR HET LUCHTLEDIGPOMPEN EN MET GAS VULLEN VAN DE LAMP, WORDT HET BINNENWERK IN DEN BALLON GEPLAATST EN HET VOETJE MET DEN HALS SAMENGESMOLTEN 11 NADAT DE LAMP BIJ HOOGE TEMPERATUUR LUCHTLEDIG GEPOMPT IS, WORDT ZIJ MET EEN ZUIVER GAS (ARGON OF STIKSTOF) GEVULD EN AFGESMOLTEN 12 GOLIATH-HULS 13 DE PHILIPS-HALFWATTLAMP COMPLEET, GEMONTEERD MET HULS, GESTEMPELD MET FIRMANAAM, GEREED VOOR VERZENDING 14 DE NIEUWE LAMP VOOR KLEINE LICHTSTERKTE, PHILIPS "ARGA" LAMP, DIE OP DEZELFDE PRINCIPES BERUST ALS DE GROOTERE "HALFWATTLAMPEN"
FABRIEKEN TE EINDHOVEN
4000 ARBEIDERS

2. The secrets of the light bulb

The incandescent light bulb consists of a filament with a high electrical tolerance. When a large amount of current passes through it, the filament glows from the heat. To prevent the filament from burning, it is encased in an oxygen-free glass balloon. The soft light dispersed by incandescent bulbs makes them particularly suitable for electric lighting in the home.

Decades of research were needed in order to perfect this seemingly simple product.
The 'secrets' of the light bulb were in fact the most prominent reason for establishing the NatLab. Accustomed to experimental physics at the most fundamental level in the laboratory of Kamerlingh Onnes, the leading physicist Gilles Holst was initially hired to study metal filaments in glass bulbs.

The light bulb's breakthrough to the general public occurred after the First World War, when the adoption of electricity as a source of energy began increasing rapidly. The light bulb had become indispensible in daily life, and so it remained until the 'limits of growth' came into view in the last 25 years of the 20th century. Energy conservation became an urgent issue then, ushering in the demise of the relatively inefficient incandescent light bulb, in which 90%-95% of the energy is transformed into largely useless heat instead of light. The European ban on the sales of incandescent light bulbs (with the exception of Christmas lights, refrigerator lamps and other special applications) took effect in September 2012. More efficient forms of lighting are the way of the future.

New light

In 1879, the American inventor Thomas Alva Edison and his English colleague Joseph Swan had each conceived a unique way to produce practical incandescent light bulbs. One noticeable difference between the two designs was that Swan's earliest filament had been marked by a characteristic curl, in contrast to the one developed by Edison. Swan used chemically treated and carbonised cotton as a filament, while Edison used carbonised bamboo.

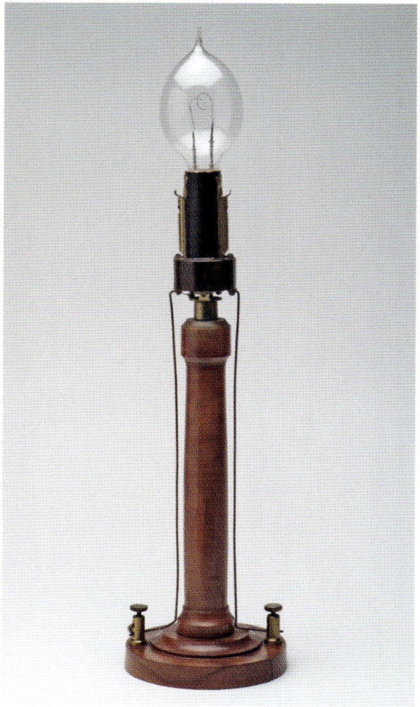

The incandescent light bulb according to Swan (left) and Edison (right

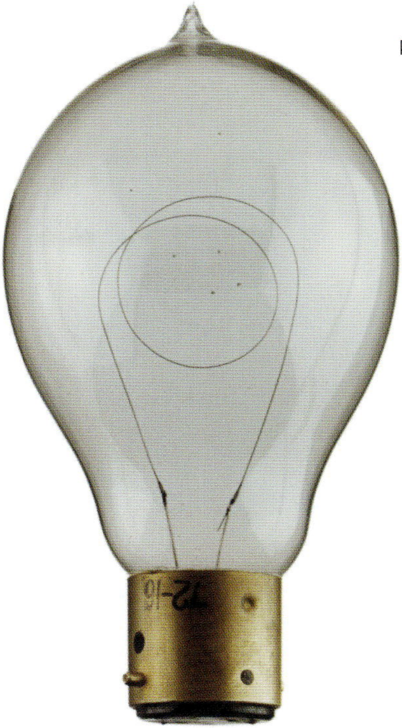

Philips carbon filament lamp, around 1892.

Competition for the gas lamp

The first lamps that Gerard Philips brought to the market in 1892 were carbon filament lamps. One difference between his design and those of Edison and Swan is that Philips did not use any organic base material (e.g. cotton or bamboo). Instead, he used carbonised cellulose. The light bulb had yet to become a mass product. The price was high, and most cities did not yet have electricity networks. In the early days, the gas lamp remained a viable (and less expensive) competitor.

The tungsten lamp

The light output of the early incandescent light bulb was very low. It improved with the introduction of filaments made out of tungsten. The high melting point of this metal (3,380 °C) allowed heating to higher temperatures, thereby increasing the light output. Tungsten filaments were made of a type of paste, which was sprayed into a thin filament under high pressure. Philips mastered this technique in 1906, and it became a success. The tungsten lamp became the foundation of the electro-technical empire that the Philips brothers had established in Eindhoven.

Energy conservation at General Electric

Around 1910, General Electric occupied an inviolable position in the field of incandescent light bulbs. In 1910, William Coolidge (1873-1975), the head of the American company's research laboratory, developed a method for drawing thin filaments from pure tungsten. This increased both the life and the light output of the light bulb.

In 1912, in the same laboratory, Irving Langmuir (1881-1957) discovered that thicker filaments wasted less energy in the form of heat and, subsequently, that a thin filament in spiral form would produce the same effect. This resulted in the half-watt lamp (the energy use is one-half watt per candle). This lamp had yet another new feature: instead of being a vacuum, the glass bulb was filled with nitrogen gas. This reduced the vaporisation of the filament and the blackening of the glass.

The half-watt lamp by Philips

Six months after its introduction by General Electric, Philips had unravelled the secret of the half-watt lamp and developed its own version, which was of surprisingly high quality.
During the First World War – when the competition had other things on their minds – Philips gained a technological advantage in the production of half-watt lamps. The application of argon as the filler gas reduced filament vaporisation even further, in addition to other effects. In the years that followed, this advantage would prove important for the company's further expansion and for the reinforcement of Philips's international position. The half-watt lamp grew into a highly profitable product for Philips.

The first patent

One important reason that Philips had for establishing the NatLab was establishing a favourable position with regard to patents.

The first patent, the application for which was submitted under Holst's name on 11 June 1914, was for an improved projection lamp.

Holst's projection lamp.

Giant light bulb

After the breakthrough with the half-watt lamp, Philips began to produce light bulbs of all types and sizes, for interior as well as exterior lighting. Automobile lighting was one important market. During a trade show, Philips drew attention with the 'Goliath'. With a capacity of 25,000 watts and a diameter of nearly a metre, Goliath was the largest light bulb in the world. It was used in lighthouses.

Lighthouse lamp, 1919.

Towards a more efficient mode of use

The quest to conserve energy is as old as the light bulb itself. The cost of energy was the primary motive until the 1980s, when the environmental aspect came into view. This lamp contains two filaments and a string. When both filaments are activated, the lamp burns at full strength. A pull on the string sets the lamp to its 'efficient' setting, in which only one of the two filaments is burning.

Presentation in the NatLab lecture hall in Strijp, 1935.

The NatLab of Gilles Holst (1914-1946)

On Thursday 23 October 1913, the *Nieuwe Rotterdamsche Courant* newspaper published the following advertisement:

Hiring: A capable young scientist with a doctorate in physics. Must be a good experimenter. Letters containing information on age, life history and references may be submitted to the Philips Gloeilampenfabrieken in Eindhoven.

Two days later, a candidate applied: Gilles Holst. At that time, Holst was working in Leiden as an assistant to Heike Kamerlingh Onnes, a pioneer in the area of cooling and a recent Nobel Prize winner. In this position, he had played an important role in the 1911 discovery of superconductivity, which is currently applied in MRI scanners. The 27-year-old Holst was invited for an interview with Gerard Philips. The two men quickly reached an agreement and, on 2 January 1914, Holst started to work on the fourth storey of the Philips factory building in Eindhoven. He was excited. In a letter to a friend, he wrote, 'I will be furnishing an entire laboratory, and I will be taking all types of measurements that will tell us the formula of the incandescent light bulb'. Known as the NatLab, this Natuurkundig Laboratorium (physics laboratory) would gain international fame and serve Philips exceptionally well.

From 1891 on, Philips had been able to fend off the competition by taking over and adapting innovations that had been developed elsewhere. Launching original new ideas was not a part of the strategy. This placed the company in a technologically vulnerable position that it could maintain only as long as the Netherlands had no patent law, such that Philips could copy the inventions of others without penalty. Because this was not an option in the United States, General Electric opened its own research laboratory in 1900. This decision certainly did not harm the company.

The pioneering role of General Electric had repercussions for the European market. In 1911, the American company made a deal with the German trio of AEG, Siemens & Halske and the Auergesellschaft to form the Patentgemeinschaft (patent community). This entity posed a direct threat to Philips's sales in Europe, forcing the company to venture into the American market. General Electric saw where this was going and offered licences to Philips as well, in addition to ensuring that the restrictions imposed by the Patentgemeinschaft were loosened. It was during the negotiations with General Electric that Gerard and Anton concluded that their dependence on the knowledge of other companies (including patents) was accompanied by serious risks. The re-introduction of a patent law in the Netherlands (after 43 years) made the matter even more urgent.

Philips had a major interest in building up its own patent portfolio, so a Philips research laboratory was realised to make this possible.

When Gilles Holst reported to Eindhoven on 2 January, he received a dual assignment from Gerard Philips: establishing a physics laboratory in Eindhoven and using it to learn as much as possible about the incandescent light bulb. It was very convenient that Holst came from Leiden: Kamerlingh Onnes had been heavily involved in studying the same noble gases that Philips was putting in light bulbs. Eindhoven and Leiden therefore maintained warm contact with each other. Kamerlingh Onnes had actually been responsible for the departure of Holst (and, in his wake, Ekko Oosterhuis and others). In the summer of 1914, the professor-director from Leiden had written to a colleague: 'For several years, I had been advising Philips, one of my former students from Delft, to attract promising young people with scientific training to his factory'. He continued: 'Now he is taking all of my best assistants'. In 1880-1881, Kamerlingh Onnes had been the first to teach a course in electrical engineering, with the emerging engineer Gerard Philips as one of his student. Although Holst was the first physicist in Eindhoven, he had been preceded by two chemical engineers. In the early years of Philips, Gerard had conducted his own experiments with incandescent light bulbs, having furnished the fifth storey of the factory as a small chemistry laboratory (known informally as 'Lab V') to this end. The other engineer from Delft was Lodewijk Hamburger. In 1913, he had joined the staff at the chemistry laboratory, where his interests gradually shifted towards physics. He began concentrating on electric discharges in gases, which ultimately became the topic of his dissertation, which he defended at Delft in 1917. Hamburger was the first in Eindhoven to conduct fundamental research, which was published in the form of nine scientific articles (including two with Holst as co-author). Hamburger left Philips shortly after completing his doctorate, disappointed because he had not been allowed the space to work on fluorescence.

Holst's first challenge was to become familiar with the half-watt lamp, which Philips had copied from General Electric and brought into production shortly before his arrival in Eindhoven. Hamburger's chemistry laboratory had been unable to effect any change in it, and Gerard Philips hoped that physics would be able to offer a solution. In addition to research, Holst's duties included testing, monitoring and troubleshooting. One stubborn problem

Manufacturing incandescent light bulbs, circa 1915.

involved the tendency of the inside of the light bulb to turn black due to the vaporisation of the filament. When Philips opened its own glass factory in 1915, the NatLab determined the transparency of various types of glass.

When the First World War frustrated the import of German argon and nitrogen, Philips decided to start producing these gases independently. The NatLab helped with this as well.

However, it was Holst's job to conduct innovative research. He presented his plans at a staff meeting in 1917. In addition to research on the half-watt lamp, the search for new lighting sources based on electric discharge in gases and fluorescence were important priorities. In incandescent light bulbs, electric discharges in gases were a troublesome phenomenon, but the red light in neon tubes, however, lent itself well to the purposes of advertising. Could electric discharges in gases be used for household lighting? Together with Oosterhuis, Holst conducted research on this topic, resulting in several patent applications – precisely why Philips had established the NatLab. The 1920 appointment of the German physicist Gustav Hertz was also a signal that research was being conducted in Eindhoven at an academic level. The development of radio tubes and X-ray tubes only served to reinforce this signal. The NatLab generated new products and contributed to the progress of Philips. Prior to 1922, the company had worked only with light bulbs. In that year, the relocation of the laboratory to Strijp gave the starting shot for enormous product expansion (e.g. radios, televisions, phonographs, speakers, shavers). In the early days, Holst and Oosterhuis had been the only physicists at the NatLab. By 1930, the number of academics (including engineers from Delft) had increased to around 50. From a few rooms on Emmasingel, the space available had increased to 20,000 m² after seven years in Strijp.

It was up to Holst to lead the expansion of the NatLab down the right path. Structures and procedures were developed, and he became more and more of a manager. His heart belonged to fundamental physics, however, and he did not welcome the interference from the Philips factory. Nevertheless, Holst kept a close eye on the Philips product range when selecting research topics, and he ensured proper coordination.

The people surrounding Holst had to be excellent scientists. In his NatLab he therefore provided an academic climate that made people feel that they were working in a high-level scientific environment. Holst encouraged publication in scientific journals, which reflected well on Philips, the NatLab and the individual researcher. He also organised colloquiums with renowned physicists, who informed the staff members of NatLab about new developments on the scientific front. Paul Ehrenfest, a professor of theoretical physics, made dozens of appearances in Eindhoven, accompanied by speakers from his own colloquium in Leiden.

In 1923, Albert Einstein delivered a lecture at the NatLab entitled: 'Does contemporary physics, which is based on partial differential equations, offer possibilities for solving quantum puzzles?' Although this topic does not call to mind direct associations with any Philips product, it considerably enhanced the NatLab's ability to attract academic talent. Some NatLab employees eventually returned to the academic world. Even Holst was appointed to an endowed chair at the university in Leiden in 1929.

Despite his new role as a professor, he would never forget the company. He expected his employees to generate ideas for patents (even if the patent department was unable to do anything with them, they could still be published as scientific research). In 1936, Holst established the Philips Technisch Tijdschrift (Philips Technical Review), with the goal of transferring research results to the industry (the journal was also aimed at engineers). Holst also maintained contact with other departments of Philips. There were two faces to the ideal NatLab employee: one focusing on fundamental research and the other focusing on the interest of Philips. It was not necessary for these two aspects to be united in one person. During the development of radio technology, the van der Pol group was primarily interested in theory, while the Oosterhuis group was more oriented toward practice. The tension between theory and application sometimes caused conflicts. Physicists are only human, after all. The NatLab had its share of prima donnas as well. For example, Bouwers arranged separate budgets for his X-ray group, and van der Pol (who was an expert in the area of radio tubes) enjoyed considerable leeway. Aside from the space that Holst allowed for people with strong characters, the NatLab had no hierarchy.

Board meetings with the Philips directors were held beginning in 1928. According to the minutes, Holst was none too eager to embark on the new adventures of Philips: his NatLab had its hands full with supporting the further development of existing products. He had a negative opinion concerning the potential profits of audio film, he advised Philips against expanding the radio portfolio and he estimated that the commercial exploitation of television would be relatively unlikely. His advice was to following developments in the US very closely but, at least for the time being, not to invest any time or money in a research programme within Philips. These recommendations came at the dismay of the commercial department, which was not eager to increase the distance between Philips and other countries (e.g. the US, the UK and Germany). In 1938, the NatLab would change its course with regard to television.

Between the NatLab and the production companies, there had originally been a 'test factory', in which prototypes were built and tested. The production companies gradually came to be equipped with their own laboratories, which addressed practical problems, in addition to engaging in product development. In 1936, Philips had 36 such factory laboratories. Together, they spent 3.25 million Dutch guilders, which amounted to almost 3% of the total revenues (in the same year, the NatLab budget amounted to 1.31 million guilders). The emergence of the factory laboratories automatically created more room in the NatLab for exploring new terrain. The factory laboratories, meanwhile, were far from being neglected, and their fears of an isolated NatLab that would have too little to offer proved unfounded, at least for the time being. After the Second World War, this situation changed.

Gilles Holst (left) talking with Balthasar van der Pol.

PHILIPS
RADIO
& TELEVISION
THIS EMBLEM GUIDES THE CHOICE OF MILLIO
LAMPS
THE PUREST MADE
Nicholson
Gin
We shall have
BRAVINGTONS

3. Luminous gas

Many electric technologies that are primarily a source of entertainment were originally conceived with an eye towards practical utility. The phonograph served to document spoken messages. Radio was intended as a wireless telegraph and the founders of the computer were not likely to have envisioned gaming as its most important application. The familiar appliances that help us to break through the drudgery of daily life would not be developed until later, emerging from prototypes and first-generation models.

The first inventors of gas-filled tubes were also focused on purposes of general lighting (and thus practical utility). The major advantage of glowing gas is that its output is much greater than that of the incandescent light bulb ('light without heat'). One limiting factor was that, in general, gas-filled tubes emit light in only a few characteristic wavelengths. For a long time, the successful application of fluorescent (or 'tube luminescent') lighting was limited to decorative or advertising purposes. Colourful neon and other types of tubes ushered us into a dream world and seduced us into buying a package of cigarettes or visiting a nightclub.

Ironically, these great seducers from the world of lamps would eventually be used for the most mundane of applications, thereby fulfilling the promise of an efficient, general type of lighting. Sodium lamps appeared along highways, fluorescent lamps began to light our sheds and attics. In recent decades, they have even entered our living rooms, in the form of compact fluorescent lamps.

For education and entertainment

Even in the early 19th century, it was known that lighting phenomena occur when an electrical current is passed through a low-vacuum glass tube. Around 1850, the German physicist and glassblower Heinrich Geissler made a standard product of these electric vacuum tubes. Geissler tubes became a popular item for scientific instruction and amusement. For the spectators, unfamiliar with noisy modern culture, the eerie glow offered an extraordinarily fascinating spectacle, particularly if the tubes were equipped with liquids and fluorescent minerals that lit up in various colours.

At that time, no one could have imagined that Geissler tubes would eventually form the foundation of technologies that would have far-reaching effects on daily life in the 20th century: the X-ray tube, the cathode ray tube and the gas-filled tube.

Geissler tubes.

Gustav Hertz

Unlike other laboratories (e.g. the American Bell Laboratories), the NatLab has never received a Nobel Prize for its inventions. Unfortunately, Gustav Hertz (1887-1975) had just left the company when he was awarded the Nobel Prize in Physics.

He received the prize for research that he had conducted a decade earlier with James Franck in Berlin. Both of these scientists had caused electrons to collide with mercury atoms. Their measurement data proved interesting for supporting the then still-controversial atomic model developed by Niels Bohr. It was this type of groundbreaking research that led Holst to offer Hertz a princely salary to come to the NatLab in 1920 – electrons also collide in gas-filled tubes. With such an expert in house, the underlying physics surely would become known.

Super-high-pressure mercury lamp, 1935.

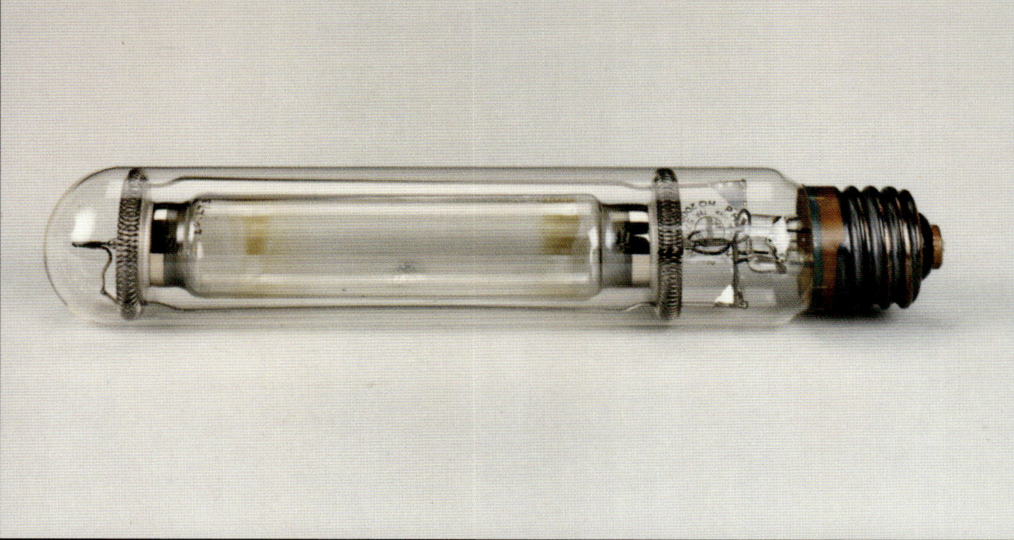

Mercury under super pressure

NatLab researchers focused primarily on studying the possibilities of gas-filled tubes containing mercury vapour. For several years, the Philips Lichttoren (Light Tower) in Eindhoven was veiled in the characteristic green light of mercury lamps. Under high pressure, mercury light becomes whiter, approaching daylight at high capacities. The water-cooled super-high-pressure mercury lamps produced by Philips had tubes measuring only 2-3 cm in length. Within these tubes, there was immense pressure amounting to hundreds of atmosphere. The light was even more intense than that of the sun. This type of lamp was applied in cameras, studios, searchlights and even lighthouses. In 1939, Schiphol Airport was equipped with 1,000-watt super-high-pressure mercury lamps.

Attracting attention with neon

In 1910, the Frenchman George Claude demonstrated his neon tube in the Grand Palais in Paris. With its seductive red colour and tubes that could be easily bent into the shape of letters, this form of lighting lent itself particularly well to advertising. This type of light was not intended to illuminate other objects, but to attract attention. Neon tubes formed a niche market. In 1923, when Anton Philips saw them with his own eyes, his attention was indeed attracted: Philips began to produce them as well.

World premiere in contrast

In 1931, Philips launched the Philora low-pressure sodium lamp. The name Philora is a combination of 'Philips' and 'aurora'. When it was turned on, the lamp emitted a reddish glow, which eventually became more yellowish, in the same way that the sunrise turns into daylight. In the characteristic yellow light of the sodium lamp, which produces a light output four times that of the incandescent light bulb, the human eye is able to perceive contrasts well.

Highways, ports and classification yards proved particularly well suited for illuminating with Philora lighting. Beginning on 1 June 1932, Philora lamps illuminated the road between Beek and Geleen: a world premiere in Limburg. Sodium lamps remained popular as street lighting.

Philora sodium lamp and the illuminated road between Beek and Geleen.

Glowing tube

In 1935, the NatLab followed the pioneering work of Osram, the German lamp company, by developing a gas-filled tube containing mercury vapour, of which the inside of the glass was coated with a fluorescent powder. The ultraviolet light emitted when electricity is discharged in the gas caused the powder to glow. This type of lamp combines a high capacity with white light.

Once Philips had recovered from the delays in technological development that it had encountered in comparison with the American manufacturers during the years of the war, the company began the large-scale production of fluorescent lamps. This fulfilled one of Holst's long-standing desires: making gas-filled lamps suitable for household use. The fluorescent lamp could not really approach the warm light of the incandescent light bulb, but it was considerably more efficient.

The first compact fluorescent lamps

In 1980, Philips introduced its compact fluorescent lamp – a miniature fluorescent tube with a fitting. Thanks to various innovations, this environmentally friendly opportunist was expected to crowd the familiar incandescent light bulb out of the spotlight. The first compact fluorescent lamps were equipped with a lighter electrical ballast.
In 1990, Philips presented an electrodeless lamp with a life of 100,000 hours. It was followed by an environmentally friendly version that could be recycled, thanks to its lower mercury content. Philips also developed a thin, flexible cold-cathode lamp.

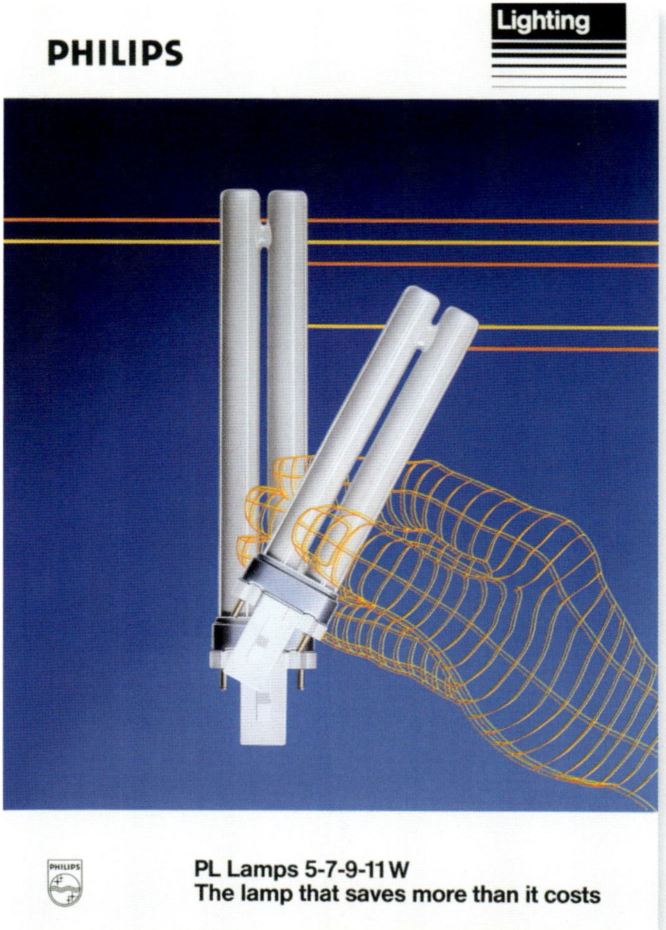

Letters in light

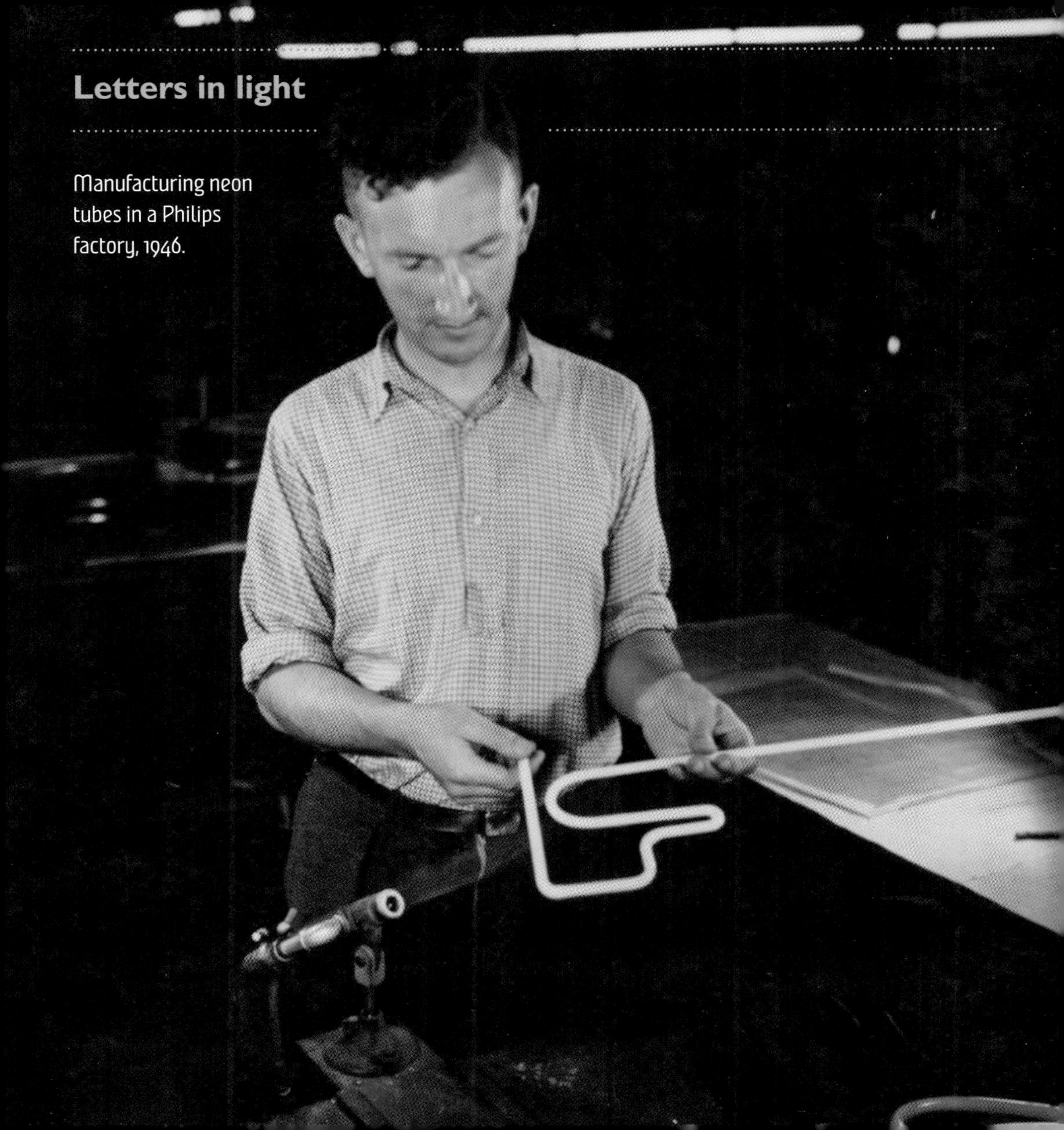

Manufacturing neon tubes in a Philips factory, 1946.

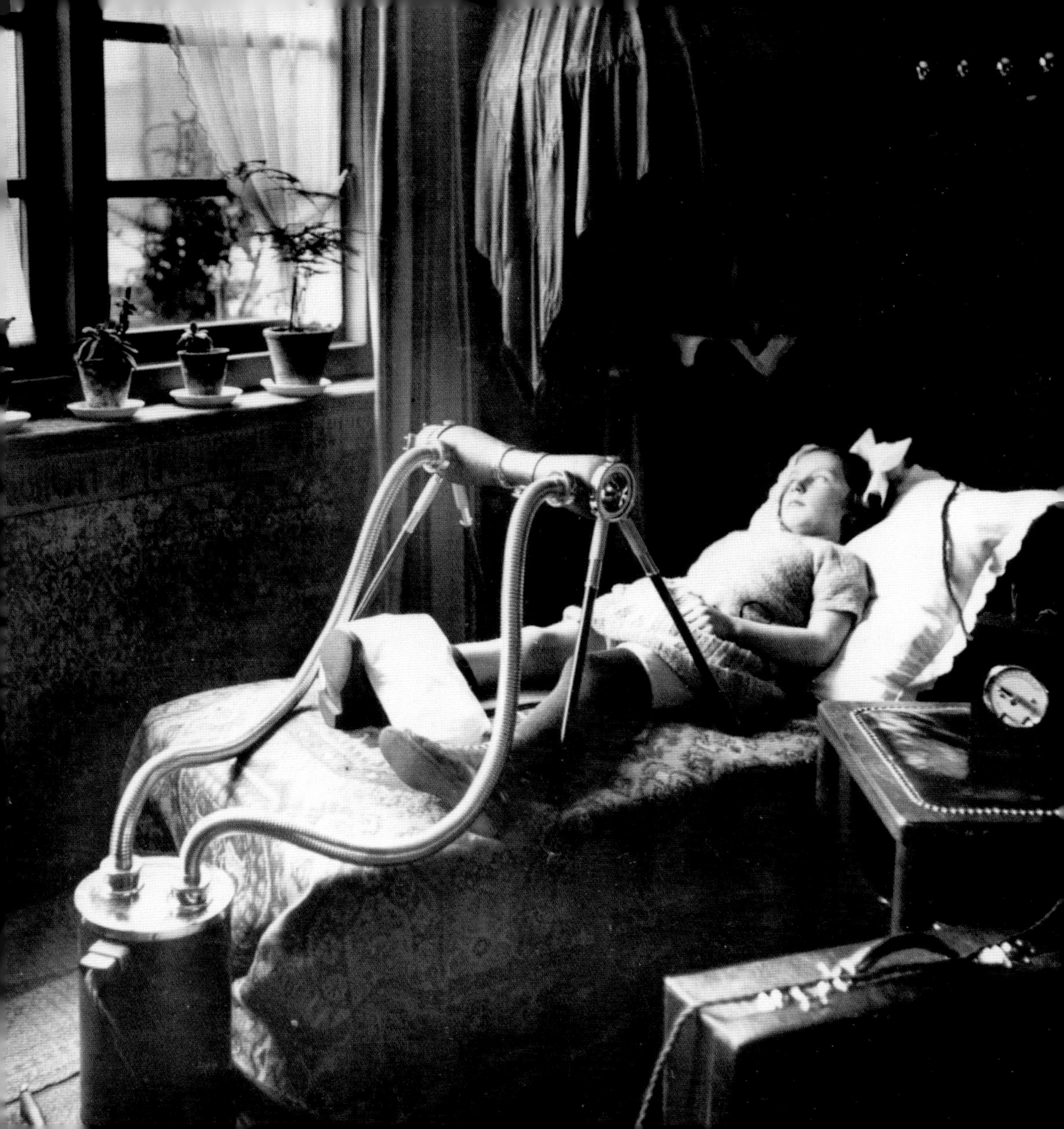

4. X-rays

Philips encountered X-rays during the First World War, when the deliveries of X-ray tubes from Germany to the Netherlands came to a standstill. Doctors turned to Eindhoven to ask whether their broken tubes could be repaired. Philips had considerable experience with glass and vacuum technology, in addition to a great deal of knowledge about materials.

Beginning in 1918, Philips was once again producing something other than lamps – X-ray tubes – albeit on a small scale. In particular, NatLab researcher Albert Bouwers was responsible for many interesting innovations in the X-ray tube, which secured a firm position in the market for Philips. This marked the beginning of an expanding range of increasingly diversified and advanced medical products, which have now become of vital importance to the company.

For a long time, the X-ray department was not profitable. The relatively small group of professional customers, each of whom had specific demands for the tubes, blocked the path to mass production. For Anton Philips, the importance of the X-ray tube lay primarily in the prestige that this service provided to high-level professionals. It made him feel good to be able to contribute to the well-being of people.

Portable Metalix X-ray machine, 1928.

Wilhelm Röntgen, pioneer of radiology

Wilhelm Röntgen (1845-1923) was the son of a German father and a Dutch mother. He spent the greatest portion of his youth in Apeldoorn and then in Utrecht. Because he did not have the diplomas required for admission to a university in the Netherlands, he went to Zurich (where no diploma was required) and began a career as a physicist in Germany. In 1895, Röntgen stumbled upon the discovery that electric discharges in a low-vacuum glass tube (cathode ray tube) caused a fluorescent plate at a distance outside of the tube to light up. The mysterious rays responsible for this phenomenon had a high capacity for penetration, and could even pass through tissue. Röntgen soon observed that these rays (Röntgen rays or X-rays) could display the bones of his fingers, which the rays could not penetrate, as shadows on a light-sensitive plate. This was the beginning of radiology.

An inventor with allure: Albert Bouwers

Albert Bouwers (1893-1972) was the creative brain behind the X-ray programme at Philips. He made his own, independent position within the NatLab, where he had started as a young researcher who had not even completed his doctorate yet. Bouwers was the only one with a private secretary (even Holst did not have one, as he was apparently 'scared to death' of them). One of his employees referred to him as a 'grand-seigneur'. Bouwers' creativity brought Philips the Metalix tube and the Rotalix tube (see the following pages). His obstinacy led him to consider commercial matters as subordinate to technological novelty. Before the production of new X-ray equipment had started in earnest, he had already developed the next innovation. In 1941, Bouwers left Philips for the Optische Industrie de Oude Delft (Optical Industry Old Delft) company.

Stronger radiation

Physicians soon discovered that X-ray radiation could pose a health hazard. Doctors working with X-ray equipment on a regular basis needed to be protected from the radiation. In the Metalix tube, a large portion of the wall is made of metal, instead of glass. It is surrounded by a layer of lead that suppresses the radiation that the tube does not emit in the desired direction. The radiation is able to leave the tube only through a small window. This powerful, concentrated radiation allowed the first images of the heart, lungs and stomach. From its introduction, the Metalix tube was enthusiastically received and embraced by doctors and the industry.

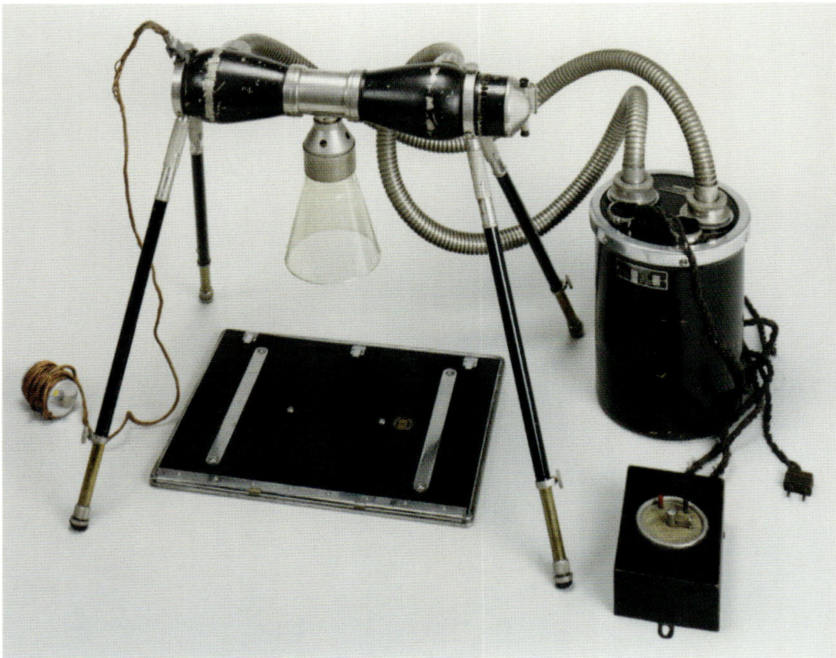

Metalix X-ray appliance, 1924.

Portable X-rays

Another advantage offered by the Metalix was that it was compacter than conventional tubes. In 1928, Philips started producing portable X-ray appliances. The Metalix Junior made it possible for doctors to make diagnoses at the bedside.

Remarkably, radiologists were not particularly impressed with this mobile X-ray appliance. They feared competition from doctors who were not competent to make judgements.

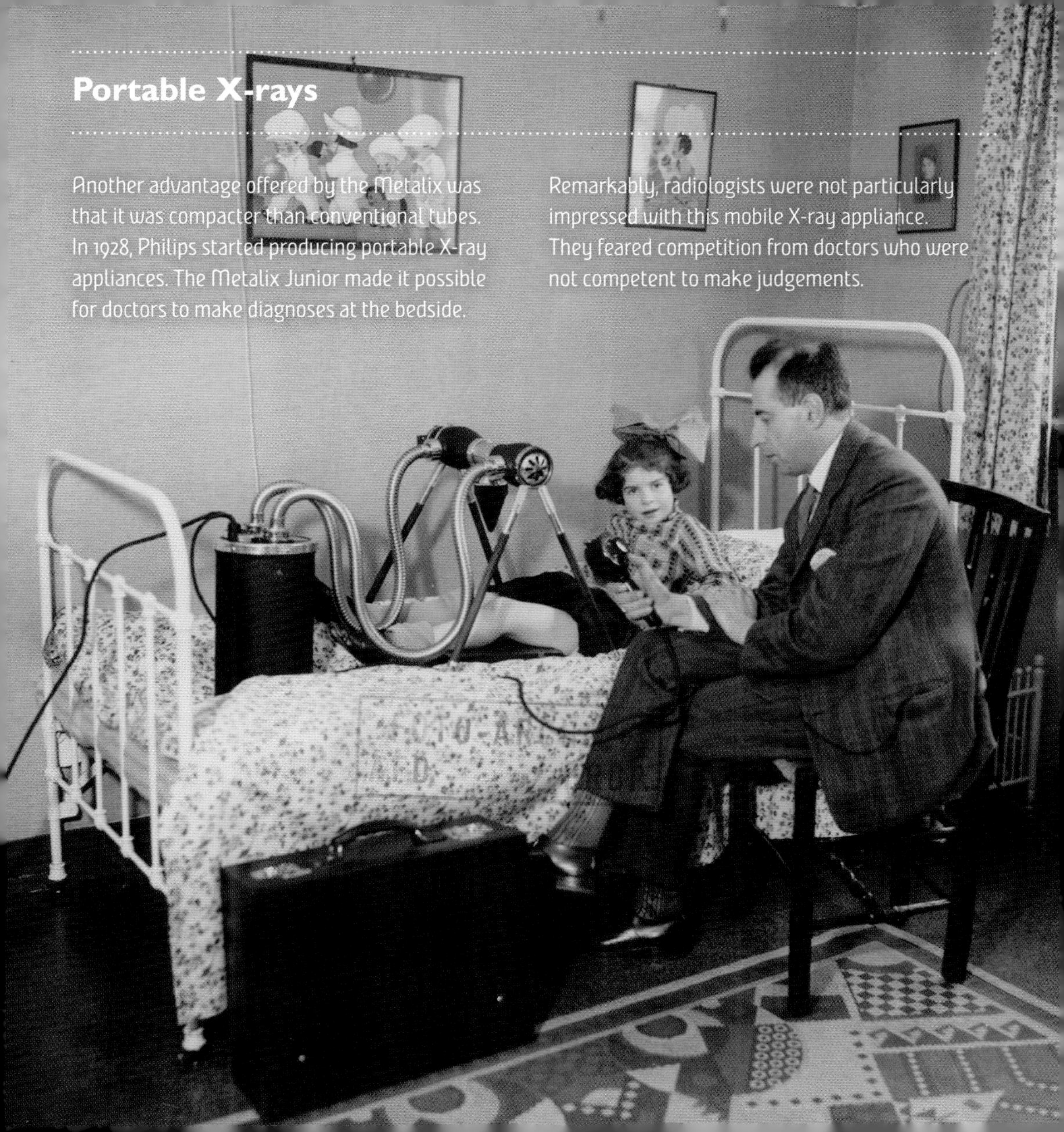

Rotalix

The invention that Bouwers developed in 1927 combines the design of the Metalix tube with the application of a rotating anode – the positively charged electrode that receives the electron radiation transmitted by the cathode. Although the rotating anode was first described in 1898, previous attempts to use it in practice had been unsuccessful. Because of the rotation, the parts of the anode that were exposed to the intense electron bundle were continuously alternating, making them less likely to overheat. This made it possible to use a higher radiation intensity, which produced sharper images.

Rotalix X-ray tube.

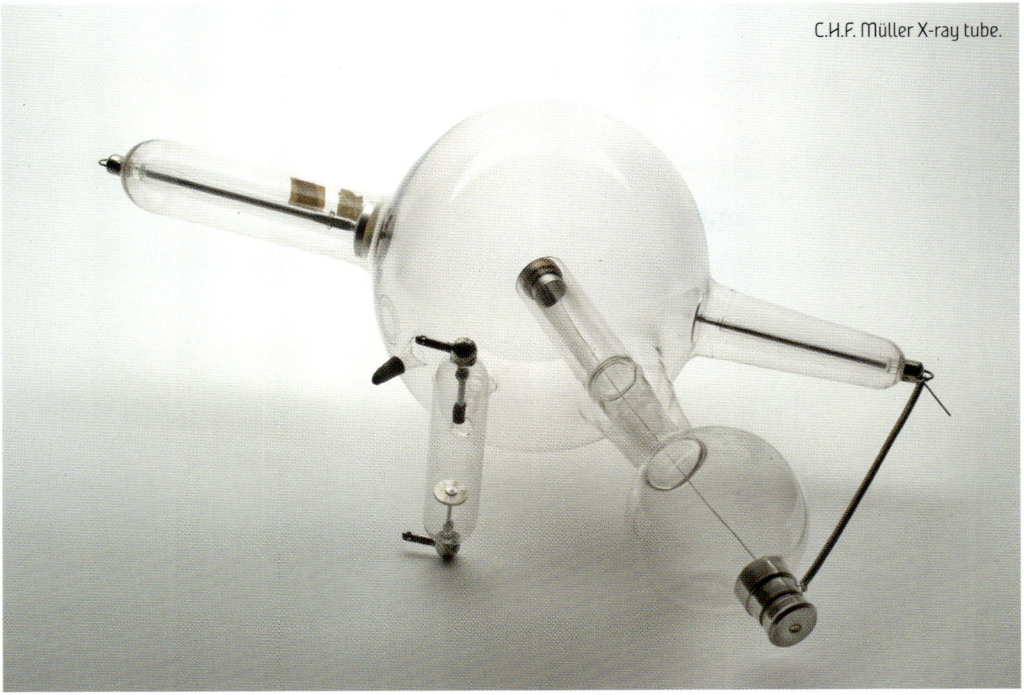

C.H.F. Müller X-ray tube.

Hamburg

The sale of X-ray tunes to a small group of demanding customers was quite different from marketing mass products (e.g. light bulbs). Because Philips itself did not possess the necessary expertise, it bought the C.H.F. Müller firm in Hamburg (which had previously been a major competitor) in 1927. The Müller company had been very clever in selling its X-ray tubes, and its profits would provide the foundation for the research laboratory that Philips established in Hamburg in 1957.

Travelling X-rays

At the initiative of the G.C.E. Burger, the director of Corporate Health Services, and with permission from Anton Philips, the Philips company began using X-rays to examine its employees for signs of tuberculosis in the lungs. The testing programme was gradually extended to include the relatives of Philips employees and the pupils of the Philips schools. Other companies followed, and the testing eventually resulted in national campaigns that would reach millions of people in the Netherlands after the Second World War. This was certainly not bad for business.

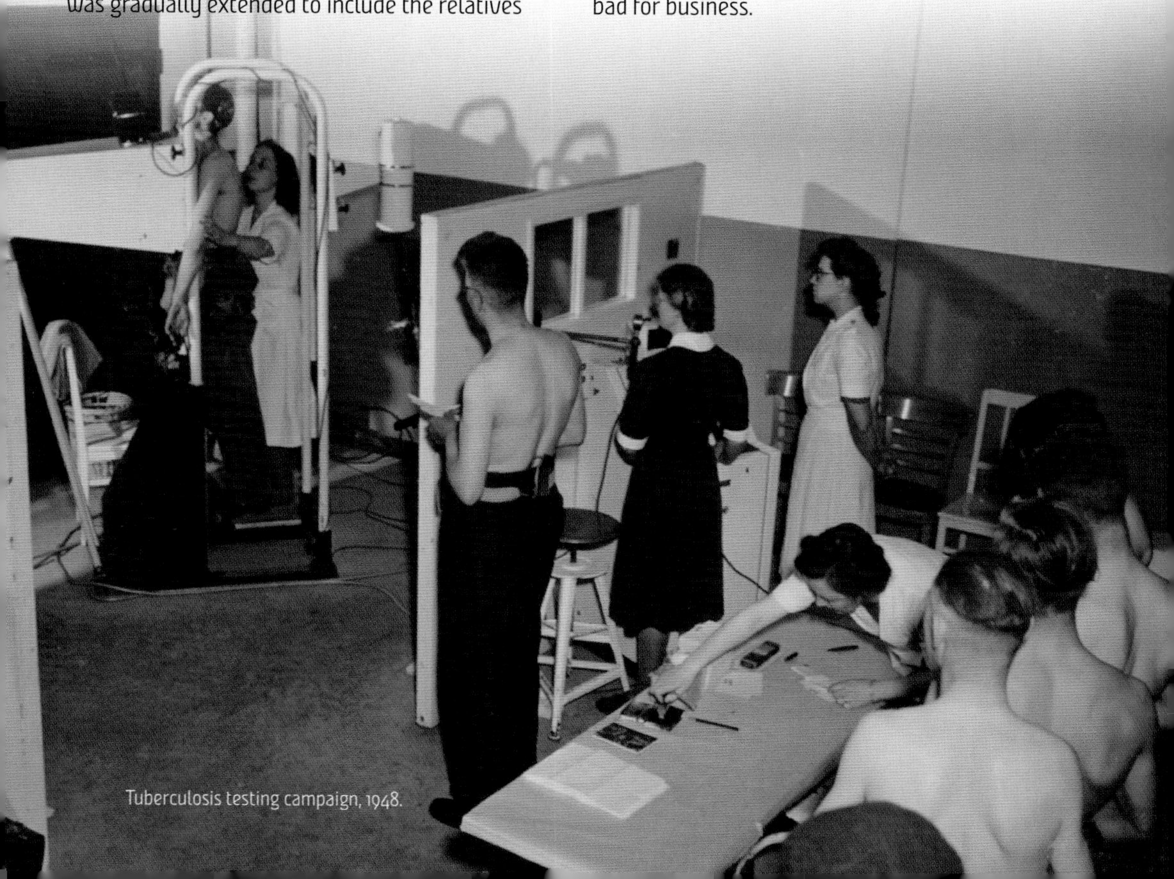

Tuberculosis testing campaign, 1948.

The iron lung

In the 1930s, a remarkable medical appliance emerged that was not directly related to X-rays: the iron lung. This appliance kept patients (particularly those with polio) alive when their respiratory muscles had been compromised. The iron lung is actually a large pressure chamber. A bellows mounted on the underside causes the air pressure to rise and fall in alternation. The chest of the patient, who was enclosed up to the neck in the appliance, was first pressed inward and then allowed to re-expand, thus maintaining respiration mechanically. In some cases, a patient would remain in an iron lung for months.

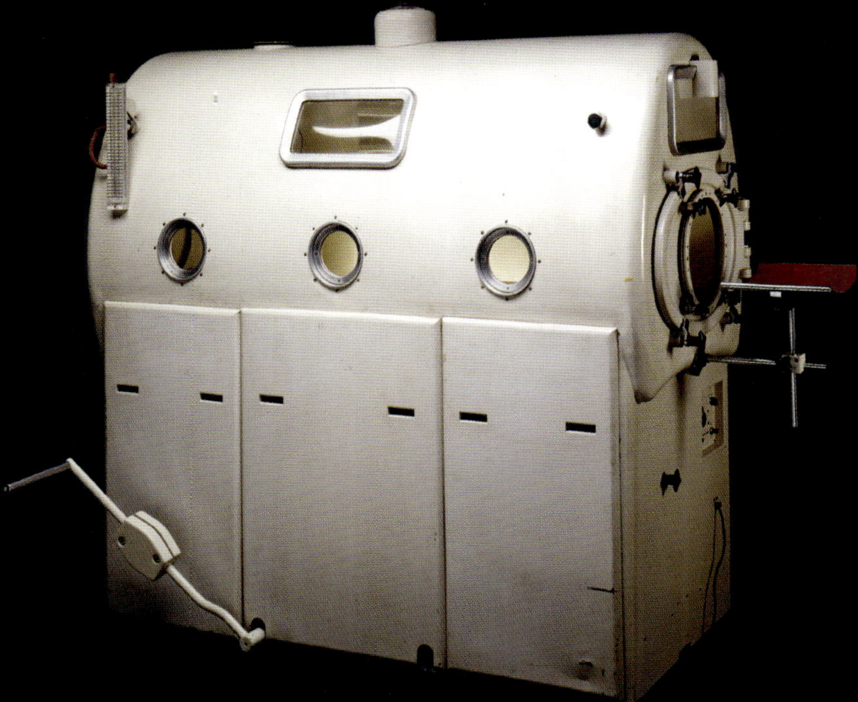

Iron lung.

5. Radio: from amateur operators to a mass medium

In 1927, Philips presented its first radio-reception set. One year later, the profits from these appliances, along with the radio tubes that the company had already been manufacturing, equalled those of the incandescent light bulbs and related products. Radio was the driving force behind the enormous expansion that Philips experienced in the second half of the 1920s. For one thing, personnel numbers quadrupled. A similar situation occurred again in the 1950s, with the advent of television.

Radio originally had nothing to do with electronics encased in glass. Philips had little reason to be involved. Radio technology, which was first applied by the Italian Guglielmo Marconi, was used as a wireless telegraph. Rather than transmitting them through a cable, messages in Morse code were sent to the receiver through the air. This was particularly convenient on ships, and it was widely used in the military as a means of communication during the First World War. The sender created signals with powerful spark discharges, and the receiver had an antenna that was incorporated into an electric circuit.

Vacuum electron tubes, or 'radio lamps', made it possible to transmit clear, amplified signals. They also opened the possibility of transmitting not only messages in Morse code, but also spoken messages and music over large distances. Radio lamps made radio into a mass medium, and Philips suddenly possessed the expertise needed to become an important player in this growth market. Philips made major contributions to further technological developments, with innovations involving radio lamps, FM modulation, crystal receivers, loudspeaker technology and stereophonics.

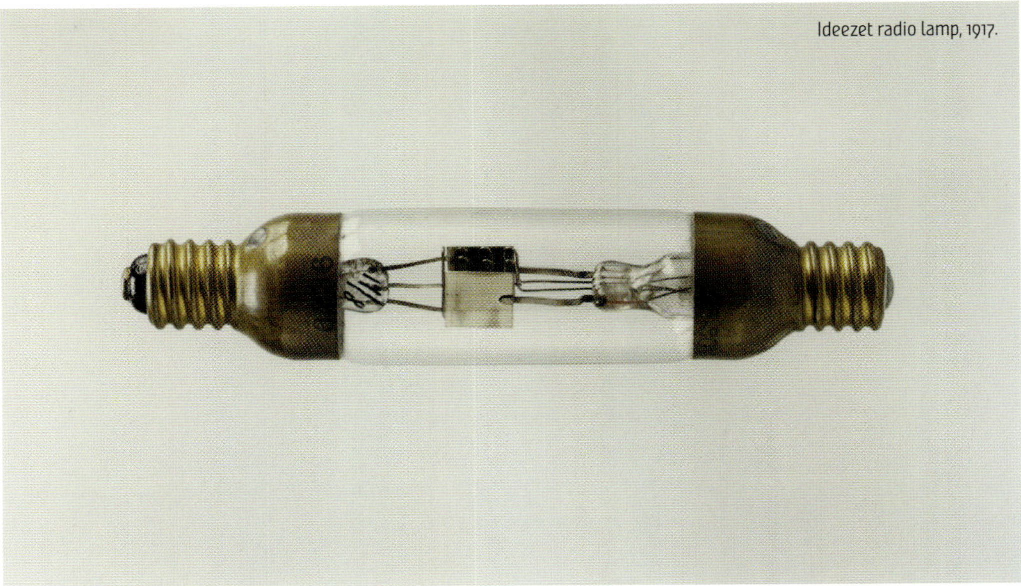

Ideezet radio lamp, 1917.

The Philips Ideezet lamp

One day in 1918, Hanso Henricus Schotanus à Steringa Idzerda (1885-1944) – known to friends as 'Idz' – paid a visit to Gerard Philips. Idzerda had been trained in Germany as an electrical engineer and designer of radio transmitters and receivers. His customers for these sets included the Dutch army. Idzerda asked Philips whether he would be able to build radio lamps, or 'three-electrode lamps' for him.

Although he expected little commercial advantage at that time, Gerard Philips took on the request as a technological challenge. The Philips Ideezet lamp was the result. In the following year, Idzerda regularly produced radio broadcasts that were popular with radio amateurs, even across national borders, thus creating the first radio broadcasting company.

Nederlandsche Seintoestellen Fabriek

The need for a Dutch national radio industry arose during the First World War, when shipping companies could no longer depend upon regular deliveries from neighbouring countries. For this reason, the Nederlandsche Seintoestellen Fabriek (Netherlands Signalling Apparatus Factory), or NSF, was established in 1918. The NSF received orders from the army as well as from commercial users (e.g. KLM), and also produced receivers for private users. The NSF brought these receiver sets to the market in 1923. With their many switches, adjustment knobs, radio lamps and coils that were attached to the exterior, they were clearly intended for radio amateurs with an interest in technology.

NSF Radiovox broadcast receivers 042 and 041.

Radio for the masses

The first Philips receiver set dates from 1927. In addition to the receiver, it included a separate power supply unit and a shell-type loudspeaker. Consumers were full of praise for its compact design and the ease of operation. This set was not a gadget for radio nerds. Instead, it was suitable for any living room. The relatively low price (still 150-175 Dutch guilders) brought the appliance within the reach of a broad public.

The Philips radio marked radio's transformation into a mass medium. The arrival of public broadcasting in the Netherlands (the establishment of VARA and KRO in 1925, VPRO in 1926 and AVRO in 1927) brought about a varied range of programme offerings. The sets sold like hotcakes, and Philips was barely able to keep up with demand.

The first Philips radio.

Radio tube with five electrodes

The first Philips radio included an important innovation developed by NatLab researcher Bernard Tellegen (1900-1990). While the original version of the radio tube, the triode, had three electrodes, and General Electric introduced the tetrode (with four electrodes) around 1920, Tellegen developed the pentode, which indeed had five electrodes. The additional electrode made it possible to amplify a larger number of frequencies while restricting the amount of interference in the amplified signal. From then on, radio sets required fewer radio tubes.

One of Philips's most important pre-war patents, the pentode would eventually be applied in almost every radio or amplifier.

Balthasar van der Pol

Balthasar van der Pol joined the ranks of the NatLab in 1922. His considerable annual salary of 12,000 Dutch guilders (he had previously earned 250 guilders per month as the curator of the Teylers Museum in Haarlem) clearly illustrates how much Philips desired to profit from this physicist's intellectual skills. Van der Pol became the theoretical head of radio research. Tellegen had developed the pentode under his supervision. Van der Pol conducted groundbreaking research on the way in which radio signals travel through the atmosphere and on FM radio. Although the latter topic was not met with much enthusiasm at first, van der Pol's work provided a good starting point for Philips when this type of radio became common after the Second World War. His most important theoretical contribution was the van der Pol oscillator for electromagnetic vibration phenomena.

To the Dutch East Indies on the short wave

For a long time, radio makers had thought that long waves were suitable for bridging long distances. When experiments demonstrated that short-wave radio could reach farther, the NatLab radio researchers built the crystal-driven PCJJ, a short-wave transmitter with which radio broadcasts could reach the Dutch East Indies. A wonderful PR opportunity for Philips presented itself when Queen Wilhelmina and Crown Princess Juliana came to Eindhoven on 31 May and 1 June 1927 to address the subjects in the Dutch East Indies. Shortly thereafter, Philips built a short-wave transmitter in Huizen that was the most powerful in the world at that time.

Mother Bell's Cookbook

All of the efforts that Philips made in the 1950s in order to acquire a leading role in television could not hide the fact that there was also a downside. It was expected that television would eventually cause serious damage to radio sales. The fact that radio was able to hold its own surprisingly well was related to two innovations: nearly interference-free FM radio and the portable transistor radio. Although the television set did supplant the radio cabinet from its central place in the living room, convenient versions of the radio acquired a place in the bedrooms of teenagers, at the beach and at construction sites. In 1954, Philips began using transistors in its radios, thus setting out along the path towards 'miniaturisation'. In 1952, the company had gained access to the necessary knowledge during the Transistor Technology Symposium that had been organised by Bell Laboratories, where new technologies were revealed in great detail. The insights acquired in the symposium and the documentation distributed by Bell (*Mother Bell's Cookbook*) constituted a starting point for Philips and other companies to enter the rapidly developing semiconductor industry. For access to this information, 30 companies (including Philips) had each paid $ 100,000.

The first fully transistorized Philips radio, the L3X71T from 1957.

The roller radio

With a design targeted at young people, the 'roller radio' pictured here was a commercial success in the 1980s. The likelihood of further revolutionary technological innovations in the field of radio had dwindled. Market share depended largely upon creativity in the areas of design and marketing.

Casimir and fundamental research (1946-1972)

Although Gilles Holst retired in 1946, he would continue as a commissioner with the Philips company for another decade. In his last years as the director of research, the NatLab had entered uncharted territories, largely due to the Second World War.

During the years of the war (1940-1944), the number of researchers at the NatLab grew, but the research programme shrank. Physicists who were in danger of being arrested by the Germans and those who feared deportation or forced labour in Germany found a refuge in the NatLab. One of these physicists was Hendrik Casimir. In 1942, he came to explore Eindhoven as a precaution. Holst immediately offered him a job, and he said farewell to the Kamerlingh Onnes Laboratory in Leiden. NatLab research that was potentially interesting for the occupation forces (e.g. research on infrared vision devices or object detection) was discontinued, and topics proposed by the German authorities were either ignored or sabotaged. The other programmes simply continued as usual, and the employees of the NatLab had relatively little to do with the Germans.

Left: Casimir standing next to the model of Waalre, first pole, 1959.

The victory of the Allies gave a boost to physics. The atomic bomb and radar had proven that focused research efforts could yield spectacular results. The famous 1945 report by Vannevar Bush, *Science – The Endless Frontier*, was an American plea for more fundamental research: investment in basic research would guarantee the technological breakthroughs that society needed. Politicians and the captains of industry everywhere – including in Eindhoven – proved sensitive to this gospel of knowledge. The goal was to understand materials at the most basic level, without considering any concrete applications in Philips products.

Hendrik Casimir was the embodiment of this philosophy. In 1946, he was one of the three men to succeed Holst, together with the engineer and inventor Herre Rinia and the chemist-physicist Evert Verweij. Casimir, a brilliant physicist who had worked alongside Niels Bohr and Wolfgang Pauli and who had a great future in academia before him, garnered admiration with this step. At the end of the war, he was the rector of the Tijdelijke Academie (Temporary Academy) in Eindhoven, a makeshift university in which Philips employees delivered lectures in bars, churches, stores and workplaces, and which remained in operation until the end of 1945.

At the NatLab, Casimir had been able to continue conducting fundamental research during the war, but he had also encountered new topics that interested him, including X-ray diagnostics.

During the first years after the war, the NatLab clearly had more to offer talented scientists like Casimir than the university did. Philips colleagues in the US soon arranged for the delivery of back issues of journals to Eindhoven, foreign travel was not a problem and there was nowhere else where so many physicists could be found in such a small space. Other incentives included the luxury of a high salary, being driven around in a Chrysler and first-class air travel. Pauli would not hear of it that one of his students, '*nicht ganz dumm*' (i.e. who was not entirely stupid), would voluntarily allow himself to descend to the nether regions of industrial research. From that time on, he would address Casimir ironically as '*Herr Direktor*'. Nevertheless, Casimir remained loyal to Philips and repeatedly rejected offers of prestigious positions, including professorial appointments at Cambridge and Leiden, and a director's position at CERN, the European Organisation for Nuclear Research.

He did retain his endowed chair in Leiden and, after his retirement in 1972, he became the first President of the Koninklijke Nederlandse Akademie van Wetenschappen (Royal Netherlands Academy of Arts and Sciences).

In 1956, Casimir joined the Board of Management and became responsible for all research activities at Philips. During the Casimir period (1946-1972), Philips had the economic wind at its back. Prosperity was increasing, consumers had more to spend and, in the 1950s, the number of Philips employees doubled to 211,000 (75,000 of whom were in the Netherlands). By 1970, the number had increased to 359,000. Television sets were selling like hotcakes, accounting for one-third of sales in 1960. Philips was flourishing, and the NatLab along with it.

One aspect that required constant attention was the relationship of the NatLab to the development laboratories in the product divisions. In 1946, in order to provide more structure for the company, Philips had consolidated all of its factories into eight product divisions: Lighting, X-ray Radiation and Medical Equipment, Telecommunications, Electron Tubes, Electro-acoustics, Industrial Applications, Glass and Ceramics, and Household Appliances. Two years later, the list was supplemented by Pharmaceuticals and Chemistry (the Philips Duphar pharmaceutical factory, which was sold to Solvay in 1990).

Bombardment on 6 December 1942.

In the past, discussions concerning new products at Philips had taken place at the level of the upper management, in the presence of the factory directors and Gilles Holst. After the war, ideas were hatched in the boardrooms of the product divisions. The product divisions had control over their own development laboratories, but they had no say in the NatLab, which received its funding (amounting to 1% of sales) directly from above, from the Board of Management.

One disadvantage of this construction was that it largely prevented a mutual commitment between the product divisions and the NatLab. There were no problems in the area of troubleshooting: in many cases, employees from the two facilities maintained good informal contacts (many employees in the product divisions had begun their careers in the NatLab). One aspect that was problematic, however, was that a product division was free to ignore product-development ideas proposed by the NatLab without penalty. For its part, the NatLab was strongly oriented towards fundamental research and had little interest in the ordinary commercial interests of product divisions. This reflected an essential difference from the Holst era, during which the NatLab had occupied a hybrid position, penetrating to the core of phenomena in order to improve existing products, while making suggestions for new products based on promising research results.

In the development of radios in the 1920s, there had been close collaboration with the factory laboratories within the context of the latter aspect.

While NatLab research under Holst had always been related to a concrete product, the opposite was the case during the Casimir era. In his vision, the NatLab served as a think tank to support the long-term policies of the product divisions with regard to their product portfolios. To this end, the NatLab conducted research that offered no direct prospects for application in products. There was nothing wrong with this, as – according to the Vannevar Bush doctrine – the applications would emerge automatically. This approach also called for NatLab research to be organised according to discipline (i.e. by topic area). According to Casimir, a structure based on product divisions would be fatal to the innovative character, as that would raise the risk of introducing short-term thinking into the research.

This is how the NatLab came to conduct in-depth research on the semi-conductor silicon carbide (SiC). None of the product divisions showed any interest in this topic. Philips had nothing to do with electrical systems in rockets – the only application for which this material was suited. The idea of LED lamps based on silicon carbide also proved overly ambitious as, despite all efforts, it was impossible to grow pure crystals. Nevertheless, the topic of silicon carbide generated five doctoral dissertations and 100 scientific articles for the NatLab. The disinterest on the part of the product divisions was no reason to discontinue the research; the programme was ended because it was producing no new, scientifically interesting research results. In the case of stereophonics and laser, the NatLab had taken on these challenges early – so early, in fact, that the product divisions had no prospect of developing applications, and they therefore showed no interest. These examples provide striking illustrations of the approach of the NatLab during the Casimir period: conduct as much fundamental research as possible, with the ultimate goal of providing the product divisions with long-term product options which they had not requested.

The NatLab was always in search of new research areas. Nuclear physics, super-conduction, astrophysics – anything was possible. Topics about which sufficient knowledge already existed (e.g. electric discharge in gases) were rejected. The fact that Philips earned good money on gas-discharge lamps did not matter. The Household Appliances division also received a raw deal due to the lack of possibilities for fundamental research. In 1960, Casimir lamented his inadequate opportunities for fundamental research. In many areas, the NatLab had made useful contributions, but they had yet to achieve any major breakthrough on the order of the transistor developed by Bell Labs. Casimir despised 'practical experiments', in which tests from the scientific literature were simply repeated, and he wanted nothing to do with recreating existing technological concepts on a smaller scale. His concerns were inspired in part by Philips's 'alarmingly poor' patenting situation at that time. It would nevertheless be quite wrong to assume that the fundamental research of the NatLab yielded only meagre results. Materials research on ferrite (magnets in loudspeakers) and research on the storage of hydrogen in a lanthanum-nickel compound (rechargeable batteries) were highly successful.

The two most remarkable successes from the Casimir period were the invention of the Plumbicon (a camera tube) and LOCOS (a process for manufacturing semi-conductors for the production of integrated circuits). Whether these breakthroughs would have occurred if the NatLab researchers had enjoyed less freedom is an open question. The fact is that, during the period 1946-1972, there were many opportunities for launching new products, and Philips could afford to maintain a laboratory characterised by considerable scientific freedom. Even if this freedom led to frustration in the contacts with product divisions, what would it matter, as long as the company as a whole was flourishing?

Exposition in the Evoluon, 1967.

6. Television, an iconic product

On 26 January 1926, the British inventor John Logie Baird gave the first public demonstration of his 'televisor'. He used it to produce moving, 'live' images on a screen. The resolution of 30 vertical lines was just enough to reproduce a recognisable face. The limitation did not stop important electro-technology companies like the Radio Corporation of America (RCA) from immersing themselves in the new medium. Philips followed with great hesitation. NatLab director Holst was of the opinion that television lacked the potential to develop into a mass medium.

After the war, Philips got a second chance, which the company was eager to accept. The company took the initiative to introduce television in the Netherlands – which led to some degree of political concern. Philips was able have its own television standard (with an image structure of 625 lines) adopted in most European countries, and it developed into the corporate leader in the spectacularly expanding market for television sets, cathode ray tubes, television glass, cameras and electrical components. After radio, television was now driving Philips forward.

For decades, television defined the image of Philips (both literally and figuratively). The 2011 decision to discontinue most of the company's own activities in the area of television was thus of historical significance as well.

Philips in film

Even during the interwar period, Philips was busily working on developments in the area of film (which was then silent). Together with English inventor James Arthur Miller, the company developed a sound-recording system. The technique developed by Miller used a celluloid film coated with a thin layer of gelatine and a finishing layer. The sound waves pushed a V-shaped chisel into this layer, thus etching a vibration pattern into it. When the film was played, this pattern would be read optically and transformed into sound. Despite considerable investment, Philips was unable to introduce the Philips-Miller system, which was technically very well developed, on any large scale. Instead of sealing the fate of the silent movie, the technique would go down in history as a pre-war version of Video 2000.

Philips-Miller optical sound system, 1942.

Nipkow disk

The oldest form of television constructed its images mechanically, using a Nipkow disk with a spiral of small holes. A rotating Nipkow disk cut a moving image falling on it into slices and transmitted them in sequence electronically. On the receiver side, a lamp transformed the pulses back into a series of images that were forged into a relatively smooth whole by a second rotating disk. In the 1930s, the mechanical disk was replaced by fully electric video recording.

Nipkow disk.

Projection television

In the late 1940s, television sets were plagued by the technical impossibility of making cathode ray tubes with a diameter greater than twelve inches. Philips attempted to penetrate the American market with the 'Protelgram unit' that it had developed in-house. This unit consisted of a small but powerful cathode ray tube, combined with a mechanism that projected an enlarged image on a screen; sixteen inches was easily achieved. Because of a design flaw and the advancement of glass-pressing techniques, which eventually did make larger cathode ray tubes possible, Philips was unable to establish a firm market position for its projection television. The company quickly adopted the technique in order to make its own large cathode ray tubes. In 1953, it opened its own glass-pressing factory.

Philips Experimental Television

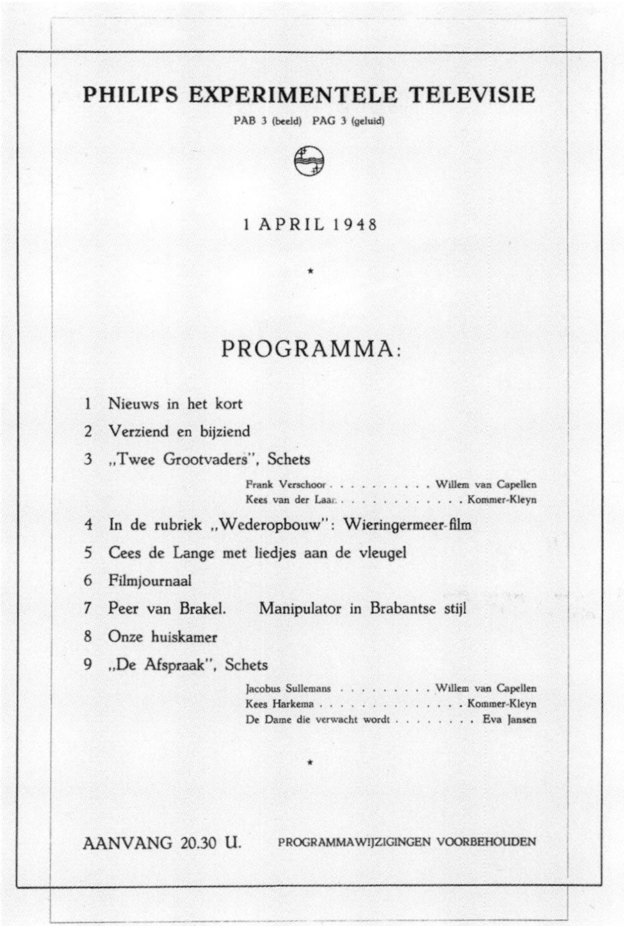

PHILIPS EXPERIMENTELE TELEVISIE

PAB 3 (beeld) PAG 3 (geluid)

1 APRIL 1948

*

PROGRAMMA:

1 Nieuws in het kort
2 Verziend en bijziend
3 „Twee Grootvaders", Schets

Frank Verschoor . . . . Willem van Capellen
Kees van der Laan . . . . Kommer-Kleyn

4 In de rubriek „Wederopbouw": Wieringermeer-film
5 Cees de Lange met liedjes aan de vleugel
6 Filmjournaal
7 Peer van Brakel. Manipulator in Brabantse stijl
8 Onze huiskamer
9 „De Afspraak", Schets

Jacobus Sullemans . . . . Willem van Capellen
Kees Harkema . . . . Kommer-Kleyn
De Dame die verwacht wordt . . . . Eva Jansen

*

AANVANG 20.30 U. PROGRAMMAWIJZIGINGEN VOORBEHOUDEN

Beginning in the spring of 1948, Philips organised a series of experimental television broadcasts. In a small studio in the NatLab, television was produced three times a week. The viewer ratings were not very impressive: 75 sets had been lent to staff members, and only a few television amateurs in Eindhoven and the surrounding areas were able to tune their sets to NatLab TV. While more than a million sets were being sold each year in the US, television was still in the early stages of development on the European mainland. Aside from Eindhoven, the only other experimental transmitter was located in Paris. Philips was resolute that it would not be pushed out of the market by English and American television builders.

Pioneer in television land

The example of Erik de Vries (1912-2004) clearly demonstrates that not all of the researchers in the NatLab were hiding away in ivory towers. In the 1930s, de Vries had been involved in the television experiments in the NatLab from the beginning. The first Dutch person to appear on camera was Miss Speenhof from the administration. After the war, de Vries directed evening-long programmes for Philips Experimental Television. After the official launch of national television in 1951, de Vries was the first director of the NTS. He later directed the VARA programmes 'Pension Hommeles' (by Annie M.G. Schmidt) and 'Mies en scène' (with Mies Bouwman). In the early 1960s, de Vries became involved in the idea of a Philips PR colleague called D.A. de Korte to improve the usage of television for educational purposes. In 1963, this idea resulted in the Teleac broadcasting organisation.

Erik de Vries behind the camera in 1948.

Cathode ray tube in a doghouse

Dutch national television was launched on 21 October 1951. Because the broadcast time had originally amounted to a paltry three hours per week and the prices of television receivers were relatively high, sales were not particularly strong.

In 1950, the set pictured here, which was nicknamed 'the doghouse', would be the first that Philips would sell. The user looked at a cathode ray tube measuring 22 cm and could choose from four channels.

Plumbicon

In addition to the receiving side, the recording side of television became a cash cow for Philips. This was due to a groundbreaking innovation: the plumbicon camera tube. In the 1930s, film cameras were still using a light-sensitive layer to transform light images into electric signals. Philips successfully introduced lead oxide as a light-sensitive material. With this material, even a low light intensity was sufficient to generate high-resolution television images. Colour cameras without plumbicons were inconceivable.

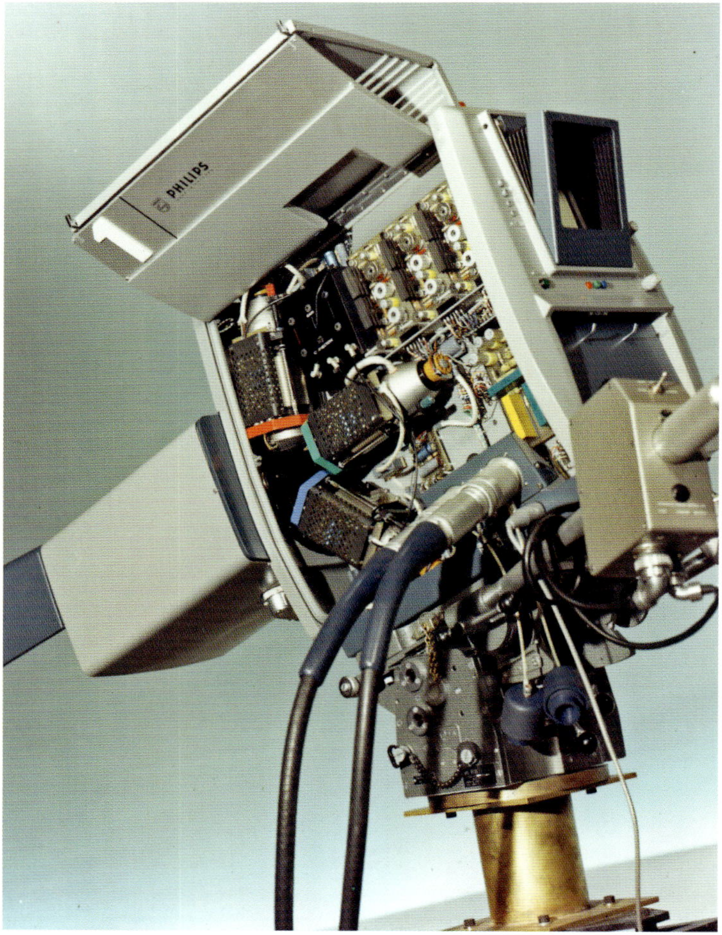

Camera with plumbicons.

Commercial colours

The development of television was like a two-stage rocket. In the 1960s, just as the explosive expansion of the market for black-and-white television sets began to taper off, the colour television appeared on the stage. This was a dream scenario for electronics firms. Philips held its first demonstrations with colour televisions in the mid-1950s. The 1964 behemoth pictured here was the first commercial colour television made by Philips. The set was intended for Canadian viewers, as television broadcasts in colour would not begin in the Netherlands until 1967. Test broadcasting began three years earlier from Eindhoven, which was then the only city in Europe to have colour television.

A total viewing experience

In the 21st century, technology, design and marketing alone are not enough to ensure sales for a product. Philips Research is a leader in cognitive consumer research, which studies how people experience and process information. This psychological view of technology led to the production of Ambilight, a soft glow behind the television set that follows the colour and clarity of the images being shown, thereby immersing the viewer in a 'total viewing experience'.

Ambilight television.

PHILIPS

7. Musical experiments

Between 1956 and 1960, Room 306 of the NatLab expanded into a leading centre for electronic music. Various composers came there to experiment with new forms of music. This unusual activity for an industrial-scientific laboratory was an artistic outgrowth of regular research on audio vibrations and acoustics. The signal generators, amplifiers, loudspeakers and tape recorders that were used in this research could also be used to make music.

The detour into music was rooted in high-minded ideals. At that time, there was a prevailing fear that the rise of technology might be accompanied by the downfall of art and human creativity. People were seeking ways to reduce the gap between art and technology. The cross-pollination between engineers, artists and industry was a revolutionary new phenomenon that was expected to raise both art and technology to a higher plane. The artistic input provided human warmth to cold technology, and artists could explore new technological possibilities to identify new art forms. Just as collaboration with the scientific world had gained scientific status for Philips and the NatLab, experiments with electronic music were expected to accomplish a similar feat in progressive artistic circles.

The climax of the avant-gardism that held Philips in its grip during this period came in 1958. In that year, the company built a pavilion on the exposition grounds of the 1958 World's Fair in Brussels. In this pavilion, images, architecture and music (including electronic music) mingled together to form a futuristic whole.

Philips Pavilion at the 1958 World's Fair in Brussels.

The art of the echo

The musical experiments had been an artistic outgrowth of research on acoustics and sound installations. Since the 1920s, researchers in the NatLab had been working on loudspeakers and techniques for the production and reproduction of sound (e.g. stereophonics). In the 1940s and 1950s, Philips provided the sound installations for major events (e.g. the Olympic Games). In 1954, under the supervision of Roelof Vermeulen (1895-1970), Philips technicians developed a way of improving the acoustics of spaces. The proper echo could be created by having sound come out of the speakers with an adjustable delay. Applications of this system included the Scala Theatre in Milan and the announcement installation at the Amsterdam Central Station.

'Stereophonic head', used in audio research.

Room 306

Philips's adventures in electronic music began in 1956, when the acoustics department made Room 306 in the NatLab available to Henk Badings (1907-1987), who composed the music for the ballet *Cain and Abel* there. His example was followed by other composers and ultimately even by the employees of the NatLab. Room 306 became a studio full of valve amplifiers, loudspeakers and signal generators. Tape recorders were used to make 'samples' by simply cutting out clips of tape with recorded sound and piecing them together in 'loops'. The NatLab musicians did not use such pre-war electric instruments as the Theremin and the Hammond organ, and they did not yet have access to synthesisers and samplers. Room 306 thus became the flashpoint of a truly unique episode in the history of electronic music.

Dick Raaijmakers in 'Room 306'.

Dick Raaijmakers (1930-2013)

Dick Raaijmakers graduated from the conservatory in The Hague. His interest in combinations of music and technology brought him back to his birthplace of Eindhoven. Beginning in 1956, he was employed as a technical assistant in the acoustics department in the NatLab. In 1957, Raaijmakers was assigned to compose 'popular electronic' works in Room 306. He did this alone at first, and later in collaboration with jazzman Tom Dissevelt (under the stage name of 'Kid Baltan'). He also composed electronic music for television programmes and films.

After he left Philips in 1963, Raaijmakers developed a passion for musical theatre. In 1965, he came to a remarkable decision, rejecting an offer from Stanley Kubrick to provide the music for *2001: A Space Odyssey*.

Dick Raaijmakers and Tom Dissevelt.

Expo 58

The consumers of the 20th century had become accustomed to modern technology making life more comfortable. During the 1958 World's Fair in Brussels, Philips presented them with something entirely different. The Philips Pavilion was nothing other than a complete work of art, comprising architecture, poetry, film and music. Big names had signed on for the realisation of the pavilion, including the architect Le Corbusier and the highly progressive composer Edgard Varèse, who exchanged such matters as harmony and melody for 'interpolations of organised sound'. Electro-technical innovation was particularly evident in Varèse's composition *Poème électronique*, which was brought forth by a ground-breaking sound system with 425 loudspeakers. The way of the future was not reason, but poetry. Most of the visitors, however, appeared to be more disconcerted than they were moved upon leaving the multimedia spectacle, which ended with the deafening sound of a low-flying fighter jet.

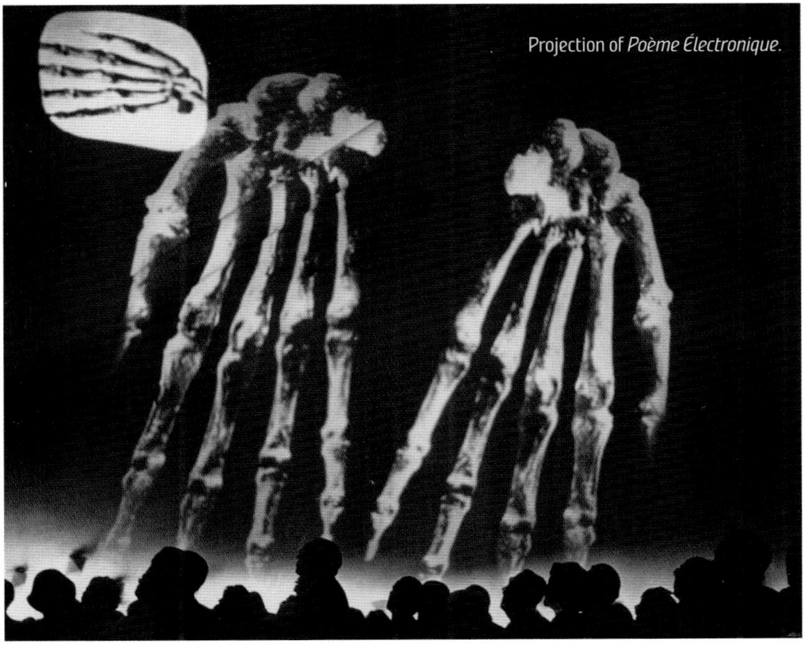
Projection of *Poème Électronique*.

Varèse in Eindhoven

After the war, the 74-year-old Edgard Varèse (1883-1965) began to use electronic music. Perhaps he thought that this would allow him to realise the 'liberation of sound'. In Eindhoven, he had access to his own studio for composing his work for the Philips Pavilion. The extent to which the gap between technology and art was closed is unclear. As it turned out, Varèse had little understanding of electrical technology. His quirky performance roused despair as well as hilarity amongst the Philips technicians. It took seven months to produce the eight-minute sound play *Poème électronique*.

Edgard Varèse with Philips technicians.

Philicorda

In addition to forging a grandiloquent connection between technology and art, the electronic music escapade had another driving motivation: the search for a new, affordable instrument for the working class. The instrument needed to sound better than an accordion, in addition to being less expensive and less voluminous than a piano and easier to play than a violin.
It was soon obvious that the electric keyboard was more suitable to this end than were electronic string instruments.
In 1962, the Philicorda was introduced: an electric organ with a range of six octaves. Thousands were sold.
An electric piano followed some time later.

PHILIPS
BALANCE
TREBLE
BASS
VOLUME
PHILIPS
STEREO

8. Records and labels

The oldest preserved sound recording features the voice of the inventor Thomas Edison. In 1877, he sang 'Mary Had a Little Lamb' into a mouthpiece with a membrane to which a small pin had been attached. The pin etched the rhythm of the sound waves onto a rotation drum covered with tin foil. After the recording was completed, the mouthpiece of this 'phonograph' could be replaced by a horn with a membrane. When the etchings on the drum were set into motion, the horn and membrane reproduced the original sound.

The gramophone player is based on the principle of a needle moving over a grooved surface and transforming the vibrating movement into sound. Until the introduction of the compact disc in 1982, this would be the most common appliance for playing recorded music.

The first gramophone players by Philips date back to the 1930s. With the opening of the Philips' Phonografische Industrie (Philips Phonographic Industry, or PPI) in 1950, the company was seriously involved in producing gramophone records. With labels including Fontana, Mercury and Polygram, Philips was one of the largest record companies in the world. In 1999, Philips discontinued its involvement in the record industry.

First Philips stereo gramophone, 1965.

Phonograph and gramophone

Despite the groundbreaking nature of Edison's experiments with tin foil, the technology had too many flaws to provide a foundation for a marketable appliance. This changed a decade later, when the American inventor started using wax cylinders. While these wax-cylinder phonographs were becoming widespread, another American, Emile Berliner, developed the principle of the gramophone, with flat disks instead of cylindrical sound carriers. The gramophone eventually conquered the wax cylinder and established a dominance that would last for half a century.

Gramophone.

Phonograph.

Spoken letters

In the late 1920s, the management of Philips wanted to expand the company's product range. One of the products for which people had high expectations was the electric gramophone player, which had been conceived by Western Electric in 1925. In addition to appliances for playing recordings, the Philigraph pictured here also appeared on the market. With the Philigraph, people could record their own records. Many 'Philigrams' (as the aluminium plates were called) bearing spoken messages found their way to the Dutch East Indies, where Dutch immigrants would listen with great emotion to news from relatives in their homeland far away.

Radio-gramophone

In the course of the 1930s, it became clear that the gramophone would not pose much competition to the radio, as had been feared. Instead, the two techniques were able to exist quite well alongside each other. This partnership was manifested in the radio-gramophone, which combined a radio and a gramophone into a single piece of furniture.

Radio-gramophone, Type 781, 1938.

LP, single, stereo

In the 1950s, the face of gramophone technology underwent a drastic transformation. It began when Columbia Records introduced the well-known 33-rpm long-playing record (LP) on the market. To circumvent the patents, RCA Victor followed with its own system: the 45-rpm record. Otherwise known as the 'single', this record had a smaller format with a large hole in the middle. The new records were made of vinyl, in contrast to the earlier 78-rpm disks, which had been made from shellac. The introduction of stereophonics took place during this period as well. The first commercial stereo record player appeared on the market in 1957. Philips followed two years later.

'Naar de speeltuin'

In 1942, Philips bought the small Amsterdam record company Hollandsche Decca. Frits Philips had the prophetic foresight that the gramophone record could still become an important article'. With the establishment of the Philips Phonografische Industrie (Philips Phonographic Industry, or PPI) in 1950, the company intensified its activities in this area considerably. Other major producers of gramophone players (RCA, EMI, Siemens) were feverishly developing relationships with record companies, and Philips could not be left behind. Gramophone records were expected to make a strongly positive contribution to the company's image. The first hit that Philips scored with its own Philips label was 'Naar de speeltuin' ('To the Playground'). In 1952, this song, sung by Heleentje van Cappelle, became the first Number 1 hit on the first hit parade in the Netherlands (broadcast by the KRO).

PPI in Baarn

LPs were packaged in Baarn, where Philips opened an office and recording studios in 1950, in order to launch the activities of the PPI.

Nana at Fontana

A private record company was somewhat of an odd element in the Eindhoven repertoire, as it did not involve a 'technical product'. The success of PPI was largely due to the record company's ability to attract the right artists and orchestras. The company was successful, and PPI experienced spectacular growth. In a period of five years, the Philips label rose to sixth place in the record-company hit parade. Introduced on the market in 1956, Philips's second label, Fontana, developed successfully as well.

Polygram

Expansion within the market for gramophone records was realised primarily through alliances, takeovers and mergers. One of PPI's most important partnerships was with the renowned label Deutsche Grammophon Gesellschaft, a subsidiary of Siemens.

In 1972, this collaboration produced Polygram. This label profited immensely from the disco craze, with such artists as the Bee Gees, ABBA and Donna Summer, as well as with such productions as *Grease* and *Saturday Night Fever*. For a brief time, Polygram was even the largest record company in the world. After a difficult period in the 1980s – the disco craze had ended – Polygram was able to recover, thanks to the compact disc. In 1999, Philips sold the record company.

Ramses Shaffy and Liesbeth List were successful as well.

PHILIPS
HIGH FIDELITY · LOW NOISE
LP 18
LONGPLAY
DP 18
Mouth & MacNeal

9. Music and video on tape

The first magnetic sound carriers did not involve the well-known but clumsy ribbon. The first 'tape', which was invented in 1898 by the Danish duo of Valdemar Poulsen and Peder Oluf Pedersen, was made of robust steel wire. When the BBC first used steel wire in 1932, the company needed no less than 3.7 km of tape in order to make a 30-minute recording. The reel weighed 35 kg. The device was placed in a separate room: if the tape were to break, it could have caused a life-threatening situation.

Several years later, the German BASF developed a paper tape coated with a layer of ferrous-oxide powder. The accompanying tape recorder was made by AEG. The paper was subsequently replaced with PVC tape. At first, Philips failed to recognise the potential of magnetic tape. In the 1930s, all of the attention in Eindhoven was focused on the Philips-Miller system, with the objective of adding sound recording to film. In the 1960s, however, Philips would set the world standard with its compact cassette.

In addition to sound, magnetic tape can also record other information. The floppy disc for the computer and the magnetic strip on the back of a bank card contain information in digital form. The videotape, which also contains images, led to one of the most painful episodes in the commercial history of Philips: the notorious Video 2000 debacle.

Tape recorder as spoils of war

At the end of the Second World War, the Americans managed to lay their hands on the tape-recorder technology that had been developed in Germany. The first commercial tape recorders were built by the Californian company Ampex.

Tape recorders, or 'magnetophones', were originally exorbitantly expensive appliances. In 1952, Philips introduced this less-expensive version on the consumer market.

Portable tape recorder EL3530.

The first cassette recorder

With its separate tapes, which had to be inserted every time, the tape recorder was not the most user-friendly appliance. In the 1960s, several companies were searching for a more convenient successor. In 1963, Philips managed to set the standard with its compact cassette: a 'pocket recorder' with audiocassettes that were 'as thick as half a pack of cigarettes'. The tape, which was less than 4 mm wide, ran at a speed of 4.75 cm/sec along a miniature record/play head. Competitors were allowed to produce the cassette recorder freely – as long as they maintained the specifications set by Philips. Competing cassette recorders like the Lear 8 Cartridge – a version with only one spool – were mercilessly pushed out of the market, and the ancient tape recorder shared the same fate.

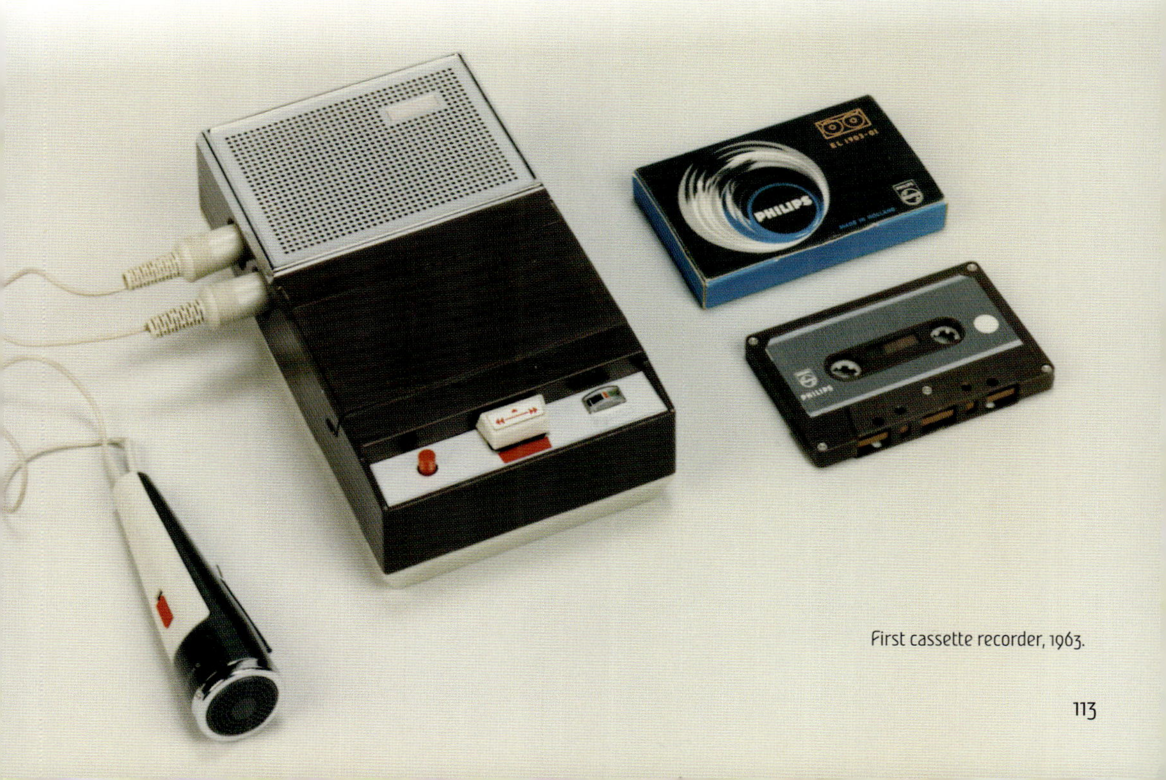

First cassette recorder, 1963.

First tape, 1963.

The cassette tape

The cassette tape is a double-sided sound carrier. When the end of the tape has been reached, the other side can be played by turning the cassette over and re-inserting it in the player. The most common (and oldest) recording material is ferrous oxide (Fe_2O_3, also known as rust). Beginning in the 1970s, chromium-dioxide (CrO_2) tapes became popular, as did 'metal' tapes (with ferrous-oxide powder), which were particularly well suited for preserving recordings for a long time. Cassette tapes usually had playing times of 60 or 90 minutes, although other versions were available as well. Examples of this included the 180-minute cassette (with ultra-thin tape) and the 46-minute cassette, corresponding to the average length of one side of an LP.

Pre-recorded tapes

If pre-recorded music tapes had not been introduced on the market, the cassette recorder would not have met with such success. These tapes were available from 1965, with audio recordings produced by Philips subsidiary Polygram. One important factor contributing to the popularity of the cassette tape came in the 1960s, with the development of Dolby noise-reduction technology.

This is not a Walkman

When Sony brought the Walkman to the market in 1980, it was obvious that the Japanese were well aware of what would appeal to modern, individualistic consumers. Such consumers wanted customised service. The Walkman made it possible for consumers to listen to their favourite music wherever they might choose. Based on the results of marketing research, Philips concluded that Europeans were not particularly enthusiastic about the Walkman, which they considered clumsy, anti-social and bad for the ears. When Sony entered this market and quickly sold tens of millions of the devices, Philips had little choice but to follow. Be careful, though: this is not a Walkman. Because that name was protected, Philips introduced its device as a 'compact portable stereo cassette player' – not quite as catchy.

Compact portable stereo cassette player D6641, 1982.

45 kilos of technology

In addition to building the first commercial tape recorder, the American company Ampex also introduced the first video recorder on the market: the Ampex VRX 1000. At $ 50,000 it was quite pricey, however, and only large television studios could afford it. With the EL 3400 (weighing in at 45 kilos), Philips brought video within the reach of smaller commercial users. As illustrated by this brochure, the company was even trying to generate interest in the device amongst 'ordinary' consumers.

First videocassette recorder, Philips N1500, 1971.

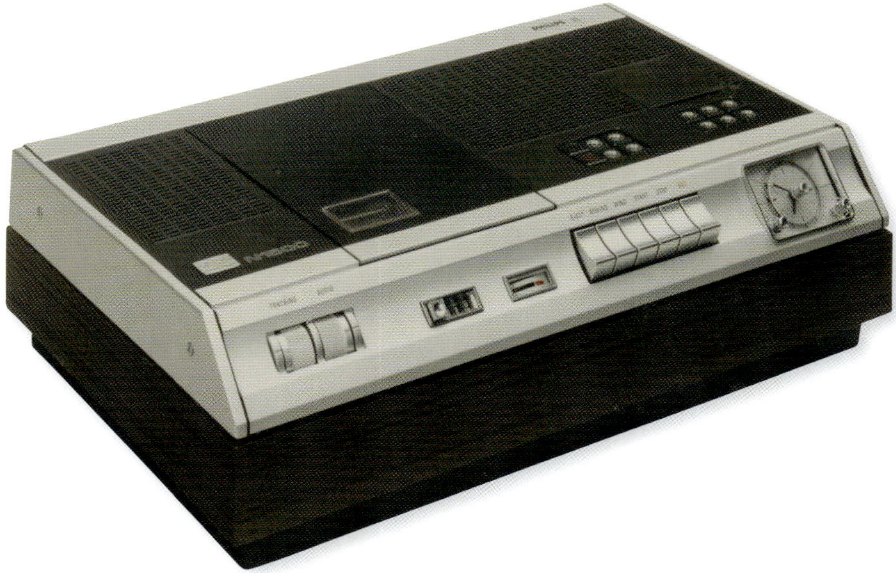

VCR

In the 1970s, the electronics giants were preparing for an intense battle for the video market. The VCR, the first compact videocassette recorder by Philips, appeared on the market in 1971. The tapes had playing times of 30, 45 or 60 minutes. It was not a commercial success. The appliance looked inelegant and broke quite easily. Nevertheless, Philips was convinced that its successor, the Video 2000, would conquer the video market, which was largely dominated by Japanese competitors.

Video fiasco

The Video 2000 was the technologically advanced showpiece that Philips expected to be its new 'money maker' in the area of consumer electronics. Its reversible cassette had a playing time of two hours on each side. 'Dynamic Track Following' ensured that the image remained sharp, even on 'pause' or 'fast forward'. The appliance could hold 26 stations in its memory, and users could program it to record five programmes up to 16 days in advance. The other side of the story was that the electronics were extremely complicated. It became evident that consumers had little interest in features that would do little more than drive up the price. The miserable failure of the Video 2000 was due to several factors, including the relatively timid way in which the device had been brought to the market in 1979. The same applied to the digital compact cassette. For example, Philips had the famous American director Robert Zemeckis (known from such films as *Forest Gump*) create a mini-film in order to promote the digital compact cassette, but subsequently lacked the courage to use the innovative result in a campaign.

Video 2000, 1979.

WASAUTOMATEN
PHILIPS

10. Philips in the home

As well as electrical appliances for sound, vision and lighting, Philips also had other domestic products to offer. Starting in the 1950s, household appliances began to appear in homes in all shapes and sizes. Anyone who did not own a Philips washing machine or refrigerator would have one of the company's irons, coffee makers or fruit juicers. Perhaps more surprising were the numerous plastic products that the company also manufactured, including artistically-designed Philite cup and saucers, its own version of Lego and even plastic toilet seats.

In the second half of the 20th century, whole generations grew up for whom Philips' all-embracing presence was as natural as soap in the bathroom or blankets on the bed. Philips was for men and women, young and old alike. When the company started to withdraw from consumer electronics, this visibility and familiar presence began to diminish. For 21st-century generations, the name Philips will never have the same ring as it did for their parents and grandparents.

Philips' proprietary plastic

At the start of the 20th century, Belgian-American inventor Leo Baekelandt (1863-1944) used a mixture of phenol and formaldehyde to create a plastic that would bear his name: Bakelite.

The material was sturdy, easy to mould and – equally importantly – affordable. Bakelite was used in all types of consumer products. Because it was also a good electrical insulator, the material was ideal for electrical and technical applications. In 1923, Philips began production of a proprietary plastic that was to be known as Philite. It was used to make loudspeaker cones and radios as well as doorhandles, serving trays and toilet locks.

Philite products, dating from around 1930-1940.

'Philips' vacuum cleaner

Anyone who believed that they were buying a Philips vacuum cleaner or refrigerator in the 1950s was actually purchasing an appliance made by another manufacturer and sold under the Philips name. In 1958, Philips started to manufacture its own vacuum cleaners and built its own manufacturing equipment for household appliances.

Coffee grinders

Even before Philips began to focus on household appliances, this electric coffee grinder from 1957, with its streamlined design and attractive price, was already a success.

Blik vacuum cleaners

In order to gain a flying start on the household electronics market, Philips took over a company based in The Hague already successful in the business: the Electrical Appliances and Metal Goods Factory, Rudolf Blik NV. This manufacturer's products included irons and spin dryers, but its popular vacuum cleaners had proved particularly successful. After the takeover, the production of vacuum cleaners was transferred to a new company known as Verenigde Stofzuigerfabrieken NV, a joint-venture between Philips and the electronics company Van der Heem.

'Tonnetje' (Little barrel), 1959.

Turbo-speed ironing

This lightweight iron was marketed to women as a 'speed iron'.

Philips in the kitchen

Alongside small household appliances, larger items began to appear in the Philips product range in the 1960s, including refrigerators, freezers, washing machines, spin dryers and dishwashers. A lack of familiarity with the techniques for manufacturing large plate-steel boxes meant that Philips had little choice but to enter the market by means of takeovers. An important step in this process was the acquisition in 1960 of a washing machine factory in Amiens and a manufacturer of white goods in Halifax. In the 1960s, most refrigerators and deep freezers were purchased from the Italian company Ignis, which was also later acquired.

First Philips dishwasher, 1960.

The first hand mixer

The speed of this first hand mixer from 1959 could be adjusted using the thumb.

Toys that stick together

In 1968, Philips developed its own toy product: Philiform. At the time, the company had experience of manufacturing electronic construction kits for slightly older children. Philiform was far from a roaring success. The bricks themselves proved difficult to disconnect from each other. The special tool supplied later failed to turn the tide.

Whirlpool

In 1988, the 'large household appliances' division became part of a joint-venture with Whirlpool, to be known as Whirlpool International. Although it was to become the largest such collaboration in the world, it also marked the start of the company's withdrawal from the market. Philips sold its stake in Whirlpool in 1991.

A new way of making coffee

The Senseo is one of Philips' recent landmark products. This 'new way of making coffee' was developed in partnership with Douwe Egberts. Douwe Egberts produced small sachets containing 7.5 g of coffee. Philips developed an appliance that could use these pods to make a cup of coffee in a consumer-friendly way in just 30 seconds. Apart from changing the coffee pods, all the user has to do is refill the water tank.

S.A.
TAXI
776 S

11. Telecoms

From as early as the 1920s, Philips had ambitions to be a serious player in telecommunications. The telecoms market was as prestigious as it was difficult. The powerful PTTs in the major countries gave preference to their own, national companies and interlopers from abroad were highly unlikely to secure orders. Philips' own market in the Netherlands was relatively small and the Dutch PTT even placed its orders for radio transmission equipment with German company Telefunken, much to the frustration of Philips. Even the telephony department fell into the hands of foreign companies.

After the war, the alliance between the Dutch PTT and Philips eventually became a reality. The two companies joined forces to repair and expand the Dutch telecommunications network. But whatever its ambitions, a place among the world leaders of telecommunications (Ericsson, Siemens and AT&T) would prove a bridge too far for Philips. Sales were far too dependent on the modest domestic market and activities later became too widely spread across the various corporate divisions.

The company's driving ambitions in the field of communication equipment and especially radar brought Philips into the world of defence. The takeover of the company Hollandse Signaal even led to an interest in fire-control systems, used for loading weapons. During the Cold War, this was a growing market, in which communication equipment and even night vision equipment was in high demand.

Telephone exchanges from Siemens

For Philips, telephony was uncharted territory. The company was therefore fortunate when it was gifted the low-voltage department of the Nederlandsche Siemens Maatschappij when enemy assets were expropriated after the war. Until that time, the company had been supplying and maintaining telephone exchanges for the PTT. Thanks to the expertise acquired from the Germans, Philips was then able to construct its own telephone exchanges, such as this UR-49. The U and R stand for J.M. Unk and N. Rodenburg, who masterminded the development of the exchange.

UR-49 telephone exchange.

Push-button telephone.

Push-button or dial

The area where Philips was most successful was in the development of smaller exchanges for domestic use. In 1961, the PTT installed a Philips automated domestic telephone system at a Shell laboratory in Rijswijk using telephones of this type. This marked the introduction of the push-button telephone to the Netherlands, although the dial remained in use for long after this.

Skype in 1974

Videotelephony was a type of Skype before its time: telephoning went hand-in-hand with pictures. Between 1974 and 1976, Philips set up a test network with 67 subscribers. It failed to lead to a spectacular breakthrough.

Television tube as a tool of war

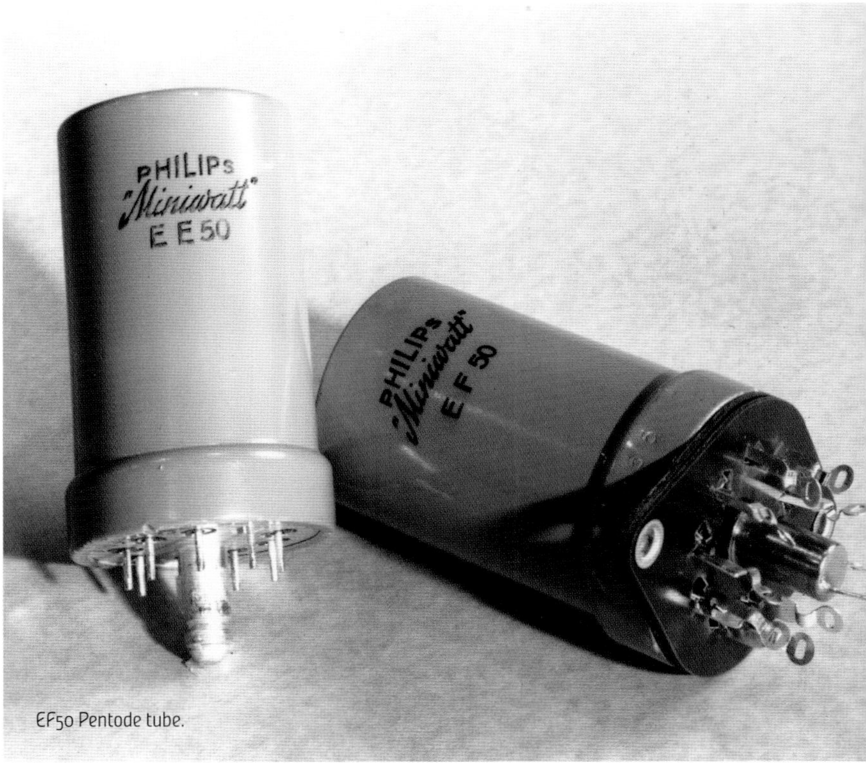

EF50 Pentode tube.

Radar equipment transmits radio waves. When these are reflected back by the target object – ships, aircraft, vehicles – it is possible to extrapolate the position, distance and speed from the echo. Like radio, radar uses receiver and transmitter tubes (or magnetrons). Radar really began to take off in the Second World War. However, Philips developed a magnetron for radar as early as 1935. An attempt to construct a radio system commissioned by the Royal Netherlands Navy in 1937 ended in failure. During the war, when UK-based Philips Mullard manufactured 40% of all British tubes, the Philips EF 50 pentode tube proved to be suitable for radar. The tube would be an instrumental part of the radar system that enabled the British to survive the Battle of Britain.

Radar on a large scale

The Philips radar group made its mark with major prestige projects. On 1 October 1951, the first large-scale port radar system began operation in IJmuiden. In the same year, Philips installed a long-distance radar system at Amsterdam's Schiphol airport. The Nieuwe Waterweg ship canal would also see radar stations established along a 30-km stretch and in 1960 the Elbe-Weser estuary was protected using Philips radar equipment.

Port radar system at IJmuiden.

Hollandse Signaal

In 1922, the N.V. Hazemeijer's Fabriek van Signaal Apparaten (Signal Equipment Factory) was established in Hengelo, a company manufacturing fire-control equipment. It was actually a subsidiary of the German company Siemens, established as a means of circumventing the ban on arms production imposed on Germany in the wake of the First World War. At the request of the Dutch government, Philips took over the company in 1948 and it was given a new name: N.V. Hollandse Signaalapparatenfabriek. The fact that fire-control systems began using radar proved to be particularly useful for Philips. In 1990, Thomson-CSF acquired Hollandse Signaal and it later became part of Thales Group.

Emergency telephones

Every Dutch person is familiar with the eye-catching yellow emergency telephones alongside motorways, but many are unaware that they were produced by Philips. The telephone kiosks installed alongside the hard shoulder in 1968 were replaced several years later by a nationwide system of emergency telephones, which unlucky motorists could use to contact the Royal Dutch Touring Club (ANWB) directly. The emergence of the mobile telephone has significantly reduced the need for this familiar place of refuge for stranded motorists. The current design dates from 1994.

Mobiles

In the 1990s, Philips missed its opportunities to develop into a major player in the rapidly-developing mobile telephony market. Although the company had the requisite knowledge and experience, it responded too late when Nokia, Motorola and Ericsson took control of the market.

Fizz, Philips' first mobile phone, 1996.

12. The science factory

In the years following the Second World War, there was a steadfast belief in the benefits that fundamental science would bring to humanity. Even in business and industry, the idea soon became widespread that impartial scientific research, intended to achieve nothing but to explore the natural world, would ultimately result in useful and even profitable applications. NatLab director Hendrik Casimir was the embodiment of this view. Under his leadership, the NatLab grew into a bastion of fundamental research that would be the envy of many a university.

As Casimir's predecessor Holst also understood, it was important to keep one's finger on the pulse of the scientific world if one wished to be a fully-fledged member of it. This is why Philips (and the NatLab in particular) was eager to be involved in state-of-the-art high-tech research projects. This enabled Philips' researchers to test their own skills and knowledge at the highest levels, acquire new expertise and develop influential contacts. Philips also provided other laboratories with specialist scientific instruments, such as electron microscopes, and standard measurement equipment, such as oscilloscopes and voltmeters.

Group photograph, NatLab, 1957.

Particle accelerators

During the war, Philips secretly started work on the construction of a cyclotron (particle accelerator). Although it was originally intended for the company's own research, when it was completed after the liberation, it was installed in Amsterdam at the Institute for Nuclear Physics Research (IKO) that used it to produce isotopes. When first commissioned in 1949, the cyclotron became the largest in Europe for a short time. Other orders quickly followed, including from the Parisian Nobel prize-winners Frédéric Pierre Joliot and Irène Joliot-Curie and from laboratories as far afield as Buenos Aires. The construction of cyclotrons provided NatLab researchers with some interesting contacts among leading scientists.

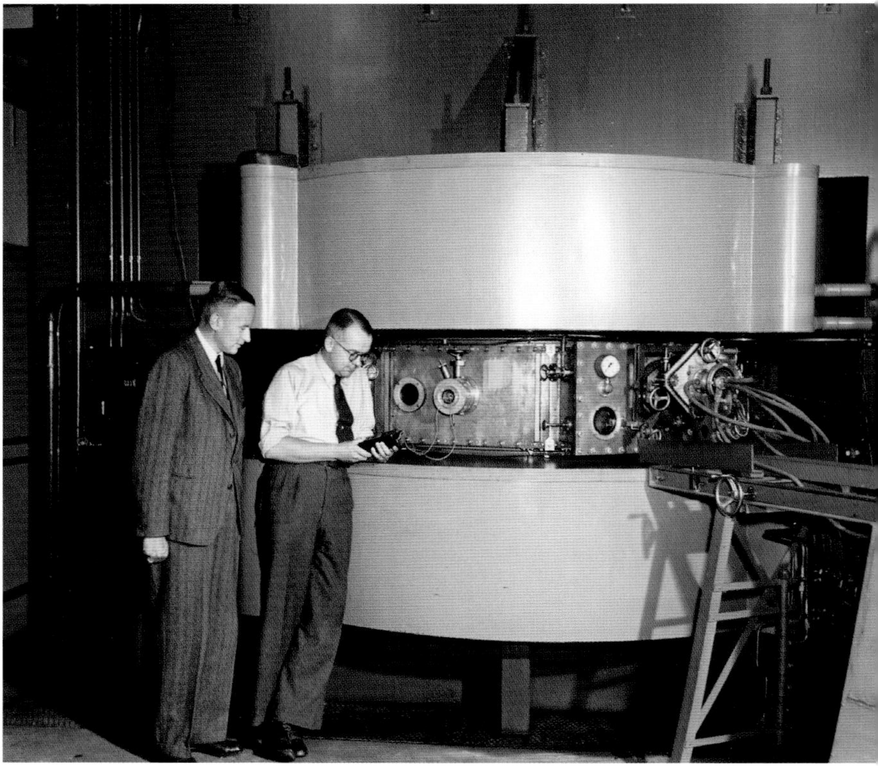

Electron microscope in times of war

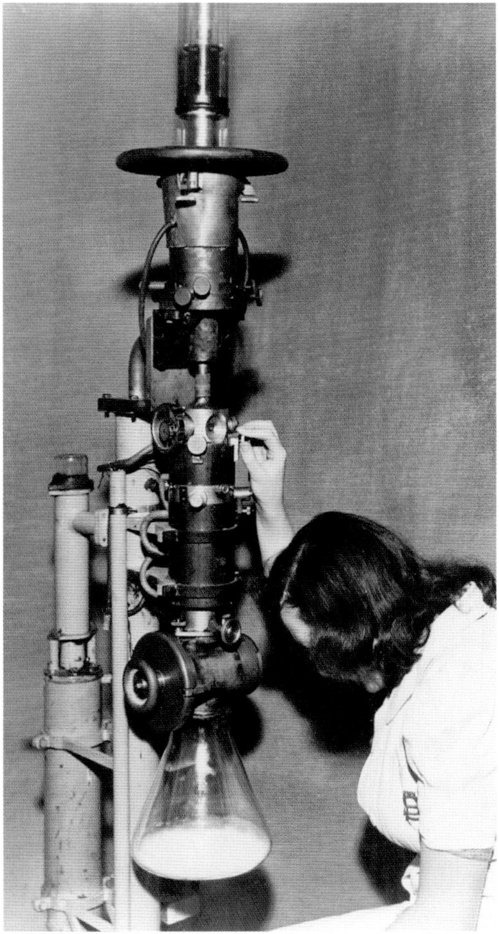

During the years of occupation, young Delft-based engineer Jan Bart le Poole (1917-1993) succeeded in building an electron microscope as part of his graduation project. This was no mean achievement: the technology that would be used to make cell nuclei visible for the very first time was still in its infancy.

Le Poole had the chance to build a second device of the same kind. The result, completed in 1944, included some important new features. Newly-added interim lenses made it possible to smoothly adjust magnification and to zoom in to the desired section at the touch of a button. The NatLab, which had already built its own electron microscope before the war, assisted Le Poole's pioneering work, both technically and financially.

Delft electron microscope in use, with Le Poole's interim lens, 1943-1944.

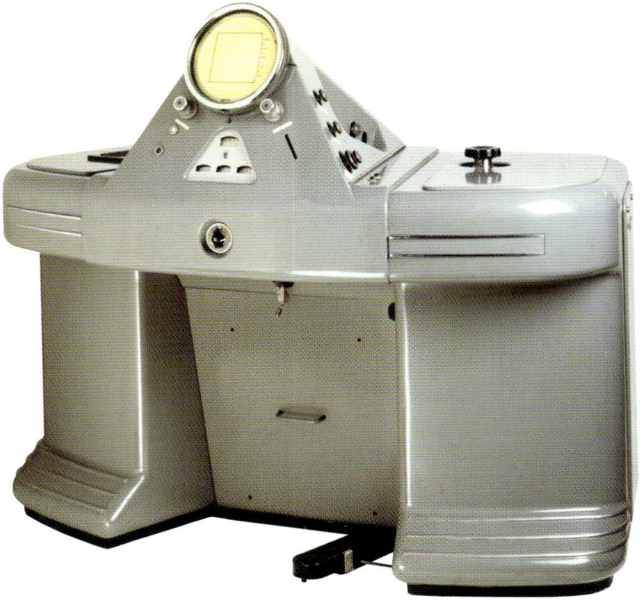

EM 100

Immediately after the war, Philips developed Le Poole's prototype into a saleable piece of equipment. In addition to Le Poole's innovations, this EM 100 stands out because of its curved shape, which enabled users to remain seated while viewing the image. The EM 100 was successful and Philips became the market leader in electron microscopy. In 1958, the EM 200 even achieved a world record by breaking the 10 Ångström (one nanometre) barrier. In 1997, Philips' Electron Optics department merged with the American firm FEI (the new company was known as FEI). This marked the end of Philips' involvement in electron microscopy.

High-voltage

This impressive high-voltage generator was installed in the famous Cavendish Laboratory in Cambridge.

Pollution detector

In the 1970s, the Netherlands saw the introduction of an advanced monitoring network for the detection of air pollution, seen to be an increasing problem at that time. The Dutch National Institute for Public Health (RIV) was responsible for running the network. Philips provided the equipment and arranged the transmission of data between the monitoring points and the RIV headquarters in Bilthoven. The very first generation of air pollution detectors measured concentrations of sulphur dioxide in the air. The Dutch landscape soon became littered with these 'sniffing posts', as they quickly became known in the Netherlands. Later generations also recorded levels of nitrogen monoxide, nitrogen dioxide, carbon monoxide and ozone.

Philips in space

In alliance with the universities of Utrecht and Groningen and aircraft manufacturer Fokker-VFW, Philips became involved in the first real Dutch space travel project at the start of the 1970s: the Astronomic Dutch Satellite (ANS). Philips supplied the technology for determining where the satellite would be positioned, a system for adjusting the satellite's position, an on-board computer that could be programmed from Earth and the electricity supply.

The satellite was launched into space by NASA in 1974 and spent almost two years measuring more than 6,000 sources of ultraviolet and X-ray radiation in the universe, unhindered by the Earth's atmosphere.

Development of magnetic recording heads, Philips Research, 1998.

From NatLab to Philips Research (1972 - the present day)

After decades of economic prosperity, the tide started to turn at the end of the 1960s. The international monetary system began to falter and inflation reared its head: in 1962, the flipside of technological innovation was stripped bare in Rachel Carson's *Silent Spring* (a deeply influential book about the damaging environmental effects of insecticides) and in 1972 the Club of Rome issued its report entitled *The Limits to Growth*, followed immediately by the oil crisis. Dutch Prime Minister Den Uyl addressed the people in person on TV: things would never again be the same.

Philips responded to the downturn in the global economy by tightening its belt. It aimed to increase efficiency and reduce costs. Loss-making divisions were sold off, with little concern for the consequences. The customer now took centre stage: what he or she wanted was what mattered and the Philips' employees would need to be convinced of the new reality they faced, for example at specially-organised customer days.

All of this had repercussions for the NatLab. When Eduard Pannenborg succeeded Casimir in 1972, a new wind began to blow in Waalre, a town to the south of Eindhoven where a new NatLab had been built in the 1960s. Shortly after his appointment, he presented his new vision to the group heads. Pannenborg began by observing that, unlike in the early days of Philips, there was now a great deal of knowledge outside the industrial domain which could be of benefit to the NatLab. And compared to the days of the transistor (Bell Labs, 1947), this knowledge was less fundamental in nature. Despite this, Pannenborg called for Philips to retain a research laboratory that was autonomous and operated independently, even though others such as Siemens and Bell Labs had adopted a different strategy.

Pannenborg saw greater advantage to be had in 'market pull' than in the 'technology push' applied up to that stage, according to which the initiative lay with the NatLab or the development laboratories of the product divisions. What now mattered was to listen to the market. Because the days when everything had seemed possible were now long past, it was time to be more critical in selecting subjects for research. Whereas Casimir encouraged the exploration of new areas of research, Pannenborg placed the priority on making optimum use of the existing science. This was also a cheaper option. He calculated that the costs for each NatLab researcher in the period 1945-1972

Philips employees demonstrate in Eindhoven after a labour conflict, 1980.

had risen from 5,000 to 50,000 Dutch guilders per year. This research had always lacked any real awareness of cost, something which was no longer possible as a new reality took hold.

This change of direction can also be seen from the Corporate Research Conferences (CRCs), at which the NatLab and the Philips laboratories abroad (established to support Philips activities in specific countries) discussed the research agenda. In Casimir's time, these annual management meetings had always begun with a summary of the latest scientific and technological developments worldwide. Pannenborg replaced this academic part of the conference with an update on the state of affairs within the company. Conducting fundamental research in order to generate knowledge in new areas was no longer the NatLab's raison d'être. The new approach gave priority to taking advantage of existing fundamental knowledge for the product divisions, whether this had been devised within or outside of Philips. At the CRCs from then on, the product divisions were discussed one by one. What they wanted would partly determine whether to explore or even abandon areas of research, a relatively new phenomenon. In the Casimir era, there had always been fundamental questions that remain unanswered and constituted an excuse to continue the research. Under Pannenborg's watch, subjects such as the Stirling engine, futurology and biology were abandoned because of lack of interest from the product divisions. Superconductivity suffered the same fate: decades of research and still no sign of any result.

Of course, it was important not to go too far. Even in the years after Casimir, there was still room within the NatLab for fundamental research in new areas, with no obvious direct application in mind. A leopard does not easily change its spots. The leaders of the group conducting research into semiconductors complained that it was too focused on applications and commercial feasibility and too little on the long-term fundamental aspects. The call for 'a healthy dose of physics' was further encouraged by the lack of any major breakthroughs in Eindhoven at the same time as the American AT&T Bell Laboratories were winning one Nobel Prize after another. Pannenborg agreed. It was healthy to devote 20% of the research to riskier, more explorative areas, but this must always be combined with a focus on Philips' wider interests. Marketing should also have a say in the selection of those riskier areas of research.

In terms of its size, the NatLab had by now passed its peak. The new complex in Waalre had been designed for 3,000 employees, but this peaked at 2,600 at the end of the 1960s. As part of Centurion, the major cost-cutting exercise announced by Philips' boss Jan Timmer in 1990, the total research contingent (the NatLab and the laboratories abroad) had to be reduced from 4,000 to 3,300 employees. One positive consequence of this radical move was that the research in the laboratories abroad, which had always been able to operate independently, leading to overlap and waste, would now be coordinated to match the NatLab agenda. Philips Research, as it is now known, with the NatLab no longer playing the role of main laboratory, but rather being its largest component (at least for the time being) and also the location of the headquarters, has its origins in operation Centurion.

In 1989, the funding also changed. Previously, NatLab had always been allocated its budget (about 1% of Philips' annual turnover) directly 'from above', from the Executive Board. Its financial independence became a thing of the past when that very same Executive Board decided that the NatLab would henceforth have to secure two-thirds of its budget via contract research from the product divisions. When the corporate research coordinator broke the news to the NatLab management, he was met with complete silence. The move was seen as a bitter defeat and the end of independence. Furthermore, the product divisions proved to be very cost-conscious in their response to the NatLab contracts offered and unwilling to spend any more on research than was strictly necessary. However, what the move did achieve was to boost the mutual commitment between the NatLab and the product divisions, which had been sorely lacking while Casimir was at the helm. When developing the electronics for a digital audio converter, which was important for the compact disc, the NatLab and the product divisions Audio and Elcoma (Electronic Components and Materials) worked together constructively.

The positive aspect of all of these changes was that the NatLab remained intact as a separate organisation rather than being split up and divided across the product divisions, as was the trend at other companies. There were good reasons for this. Philips Research was the source of thousands of patents (a source of income that was not to be underestimated) and served as a multidisciplinary knowledge centre of which the product divisions' development labs could take advantage. The 30% corporate funding turned out to be insufficient to maintain the 'key technologies' deemed indispensable for the long-term and for 'capability management', which meant ensuring that expertise considered to be essential remained in place. In order to continue to attract new talent in times of zero or even negative growth, NatLab employees were encouraged to transfer to the product divisions (employees spent an average of seven years at the NatLab).

To keep the company on track, Royal Philips N.V. has made major changes to its activities in recent years. IC technology (the illustrious megaproject was abruptly cancelled in 1989), the home computer and even consumer electronics have slowly disappeared. Some of these activities were taken over by spin-off companies. In 1984, ASML launched a joint-venture between Philips and ASM International, and very successfully built machines for chip manufacturing. Philips' electron microscopy merged with FEI in 1997, the semiconductors division has been part of NXP Semiconductors since 2006 and in 2012 Philips entered into a joint-

Jan Timmer, Philips CEO at the time of the cost-cutting operation Centurion, presents the annual figures for 1993 at the meeting of shareholders.

venture with Chinese company TPV, which took over production of Philips TVs. At the start of 2013, Philips considered selling off its activities in audio, video, multimedia and electronics accessories to Japanese company Funai, but the deal fell through.

As a result of these moves, the modern-day Philips – and with it also Philips Research – focuses on three areas: *Healthcare*, *Consumer Lifestyle* and *Lighting*. No more CD players, computers or televisions, but MRI scanners, Senseo and LED lighting instead. The products may be different, but there is a startling continuity in the underlying technology. Philips Research has also retained its independence, on the proviso that a research success is only truly successful if it is also a business success. Philips Research (headquartered in Eindhoven, with locations in Bangalore, Briarcliff, Cambridge, Hamburg and Shanghai) employs around 1,500 staff after all the cost-cutting exercises. Its research budget continues to be around 1% of Philips' total turnover (Research & Development for the whole of Philips was 7% of the annual turnover in 2012). The Waalre site has recently been updated and extended to become High Tech Campus Eindhoven, where Philips Research and other Philips divisions have since been joined by more than a hundred institutes and businesses working on technologies and products of the future.

Since health and welfare now play such an important role within Philips, the research mission has been modified. Improving the quality of human life now takes centre stage, through the innovations that can help achieve that, made possible by new technologies. Innovations that lead to a more sustainable and healthier world. In this, Philips Research engages in what it calls 'open innovation'. Open innovation works in two directions. Outwardly, it involves Philips Research making its expertise available to third parties. These are primarily the product divisions, but it also works for third parties on contract research or by way of supplying technical facilities and providing external support. Inward open innovation involves Philips Research making use of the services of university laboratories or start-up companies across the world. Approximately 65% of Philips Research projects are carried out in alliance with universities, knowledge institutions or government bodies. Customers, suppliers or partners of Philips businesses are involved in around half of these projects.

As a result, the High Tech Campus Eindhoven has now come to be home to a photonics group that is part of AMOLF (a division of the Netherlands Organisation for Scientific Research/NWO) working closely with Philips Research. Philips Research has also joined forces with the Utrecht University Medical Centre and Eindhoven University of Technology in the field of innovative methods of diagnosis and treatment, such as the real-time irradiation of patients in an MRI scanner (not to be confused with HIFU ultrasound technology). Through all of this, Philips Research hopes to broaden its perspective and at the same time raise its profile as an attractive employer that gives talent room to grow.

At Philips, the customer now takes centre stage: the company aims to respond to customer needs, together with the challenges faced by society as a whole. Bringing an end to the increase in cardiovascular diseases, making safe and comfortable cities a reality: these are the areas that Philips is increasingly claiming as its own. The result is innovative imaging technologies using low-dose X-ray or ultrasound. Or software for replacing pacemakers that combines monitoring (using

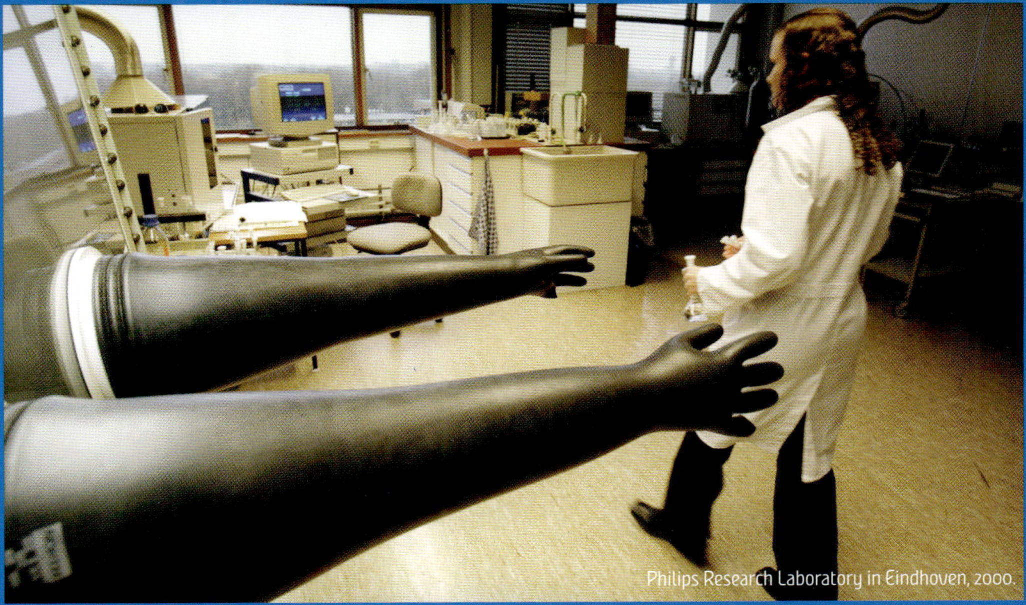
Philips Research Laboratory in Eindhoven, 2000.

an MRI scanner) with medical intervention. The challenges facing major cities concern the efficient use of energy or the intelligent application of street lighting. Even dental care offers multiple challenges that Philips is eager to tackle. The Airfloss with its micro-droplets has its origins at Philips Research.

A quick glance at the Philips products launched in 2012-2013 provides a good illustration of this change in focus. *Healthcare* continued to make progress on digital pathology and a hybrid PET/MR scanner. *Consumer Lifestyle* developed a 3-D television and Lumea Precision. And *Lighting* launched the HealWell and LumiMotion. Philips Research was involved in the development of all of these.

This is how Philips Research continues to reinvent itself to this day, supported by a rich history of a century of inventions that matter.

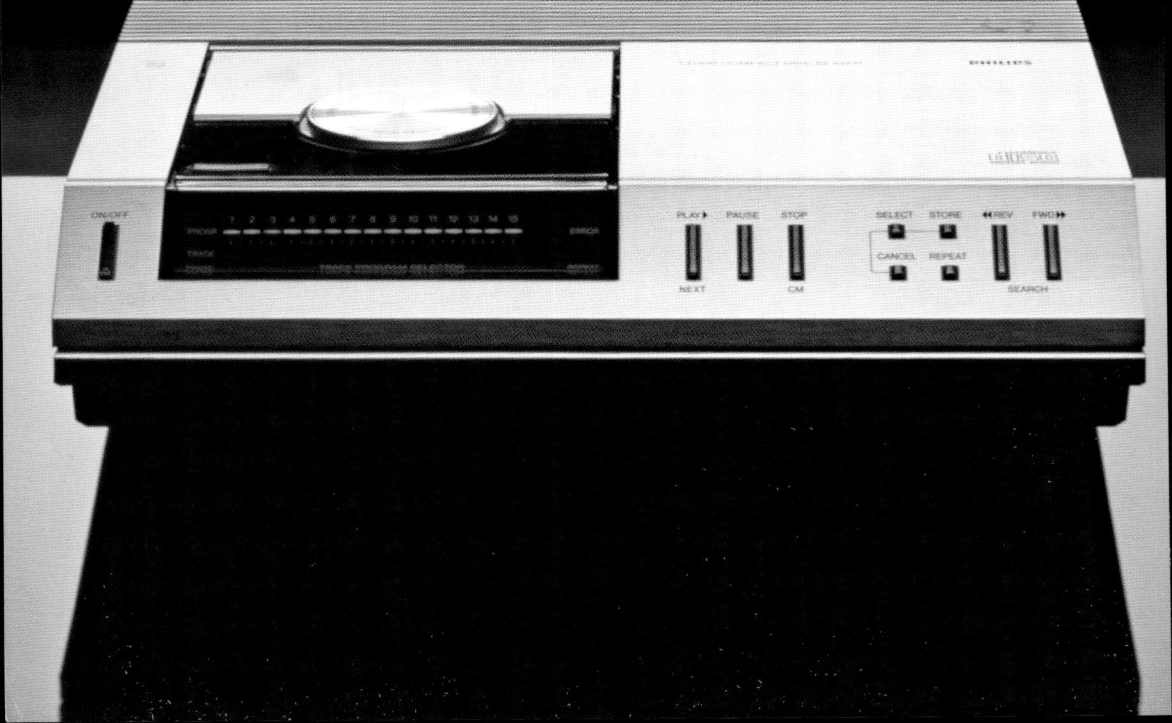
PHILIPS
ON/OFF
1 2 3 4 5 6 7 8 9 10 11 12 13 14 15
ERROR
TRACK
PLAY
PAUSE
STOP
SELECT
STORE
REV
FWD
CANCEL
REPEAT
NEXT
CM
SEARCH

13. The shiny disc

After the needle and groove, the tape and the magnetic head, in the 1980s it was the turn of the laser and the pitted disc to enter the world of sound reproduction. Philips pioneered this revolutionary development.

Almost immediately after the invention of the laser in 1958, experiments began on the storage of information on optical discs. In 1961, American David Paul Gregg patented a video disc that could be read by laser. Philips also began by focusing on the storage and display of images, which led to the development of the Video Long Play, on which images were encoded onto a disc. When this product failed, the idea emerged of using the technology for sound reproduction only. Was it not possible to produce a video disc with no images? It was indeed possible, but it called for one key modification: the sound information was no longer stored in analogue form, but digitally. The pits and lands on the compact disc provided the ones and zeros that the device converted into music. Added digital information was used to correct the errors caused by damaged pits, one of the problems that had plagued the VLP.

Thanks to its strategic alliance with Sony and some smart marketing, Philips was successful in ensuring that the compact disc almost completely superseded the gramophone record. A quarter of a century after its introduction, 200 billion discs had been sold. The heyday of the compact disc came to a halt in around the year 2000. Firstly, computers made it possible to copy CDs onto recordable CDs (which also originated from Philips and Sony) or convert them into mp3 files, after which music lovers began to download their music from the internet in large numbers.

First commercial CD player, 1982.

The video disc

In the case of the predecessor of the compact disc, the Video Long Play, short video images were encoded microscopically onto a disc measuring 30 cm in diameter. These were read by a laser, and the device converted the light signals into a stream of flowing images. This made it possible to play films or TV programmes. The VLP (or video disc) was a technical innovation devised in the NatLab. It was expected to be a major hit with consumers. In 1978, the device appeared on the American market under the name LaserVision.

Sadly, it was bought by virtually no Americans at all, partly because of the lack of an attractive range of video discs to play on it.

Major alliance with Sony

As the development of the CD continued to progress, Philips gradually realised that its competitors were also making advances. In order to prevent the launch going hand-in-hand with a battle between different systems – as was already happening with video – efforts were made to find a powerful partner in the Far East. A delegation headed to Japan with this small prototype, named 'Pinkeltje' after a tiny and much-loved character from Dutch children's literature, in order to convince major companies there to enter into business with their European competitors. Sony took the bait. Philips worked with specialists from Sony to develop the CD we know today: a disc 12 cm in diameter, made of plastic (polycarbonate) and covered with a layer of reflective aluminium on the playable side. The groove of 'pits' and 'lands' forms a spiral that is read from the inside outwards. The lands reflect the laser light and the pits almost completely black it out.

From Vivaldi to Beethoven

This compact disc featuring Vivaldi's *Four Seasons* is 11.5 cm in diameter. This is smaller than a modern compact disc. After Sony joined forces with Philips, there were some serious negotiations about technical specifications and standards. One of the bosses at Sony insisted that his favourite version of Beethoven's Ninth Symphony would fit onto a disc. This meant increasing the playing time from 60 to 74 minutes, and the diameter to 12 cm. Philips was able to determine the dimensions of the hole in the middle. The choice was not the result of any complicated reasoning. The dimension chosen was the size of an old ten Dutch guilder cent coin – try it out for yourself.

Vivaldi op 11,5 cm.

Doe Maar and Dire Straits live on CD

The compact disc had three key advantages compared to the LP: its size, its sound quality and its resistance to wear and tear. Philips had learnt some hard lessons and knew only too well that technical innovation alone would not be enough to win over consumers in the 1980s. It was all about image and emotion. In order to promote this metal disc, stars from the music world would serve as ambassadors, including conductor Herbert von Karajan, pop group Dire Straits and, in the Netherlands, Doe Maar.

Jagger in Eindhoven

The great Mick Jagger himself visited Eindhoven in order to be personally convinced of this new musical medium, on which his records would also be published. CEO Jan Timmer was on hand to explain it all.

The interactive CD-i

The compact disc went on to spawn a range of variants, some more successful than others. The CD-i was a compact disc that was played on TV. The discs contained images and sound that could be manipulated using a mouse or joystick. Consumers could play games, or even consult a digital encyclopaedia with historical sound and video excerpts, or wander through a museum. However, the CD-i faced stiff competition from a new generation of games computers on the one hand (Sony's PlayStation) and the PC on the other. The launch of the CD-i coincided with that of the CD-ROM, which significantly increased the memory capacity of the PC (compared to the floppy disk). Ultimately, the interactive blend of images sound and data envisaged by the CD-i would find its home on the PC.

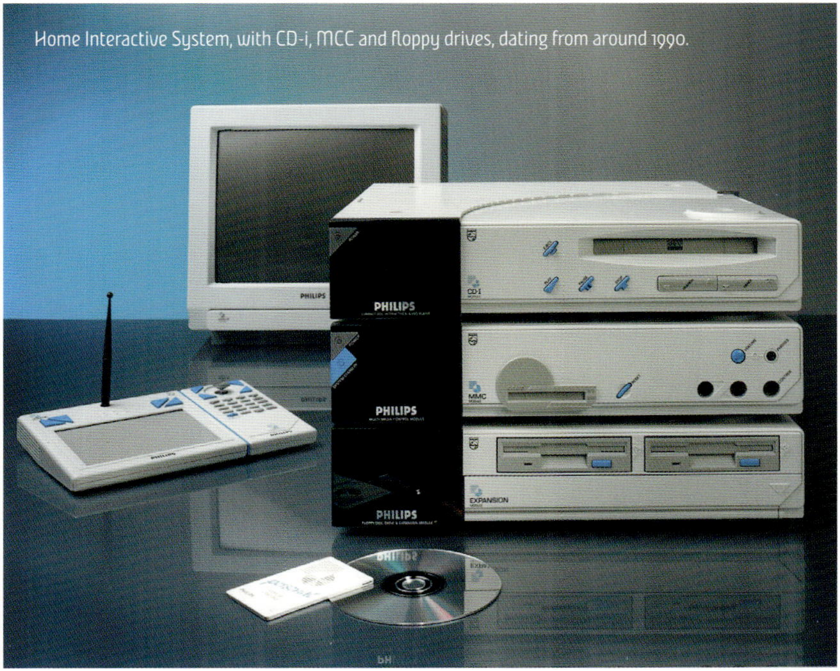

Home Interactive System, with CD-i, MCC and floppy drives, dating from around 1990.

Blu-ray

Blu-ray proved to be more successful than the CD-i. Philips collaborated on this product with Sony and Pioneer. Blu-ray uses discs that appear to be identical to compact discs. However, Blu-ray players use laser light with a shorter wavelength, enabling more information to be stored on a disc. This makes it possible to store and view films with HD-quality pictures and sound. Blu-ray was intended to be the successor to the DVD. In 2011, Philips was awarded a Technology & Engineering Emmy for its contribution to the development of the Blu-ray.

Blu-ray Player BDP 7500.

Successors to the CD

In the wake of the compact disc came numerous other products, including the CD-rewritable, CD-recordable, DVD and CD-ROM.

110 200
160 250
VOLTS
PHILIPS
The Perfect
Shaving Instrument

14. Personal Care

All three of the sectors that currently make up Philips started out from a single original technology. *Healthcare* started with the X-ray tube, *Lighting* from the light bulb and *Consumer Lifestyle* from the radio and television tube. The origins of *Personal Care*, part of *Consumer Lifestyle* are less easy to trace. On the one hand, Philips launched the Ultrasol health lamp onto the market in the 1930s, derived from its research into lighting. This was a response to new medical discoveries and the fashion for using electromagnetic radiation as a panacea for countless ailments and disorders.

On the other hand, there was the amazing success of the Philishave. No other single product has been such a stable source of income for Philips. Whether it was the 'egg' (the 1950s Philishave), its successor with the double shaver head, the next generation with three heads or the Philishave Cool Skin – all of them were money spinners. Despite this, Philips engineer Horowitz did not receive immediate acclaim for his prototype in 1939. 'We are not barbers', Anton Philips is said to have exclaimed. It was only when his son-in-law, Frans Otten, tried out the shaver – he shaved one side of his face with the Philishave and the other with an American shaver – that the senior management were convinced. In 2006, Philips replaced the famous Philishave brand name with Philips Shaver.

For a long time, personal care was not seen as a separate category. The fact that, back in 1958, sunlamps and shavers were categorised as household appliances, together with mixers and irons, reveals a lot.

Advertisement for Philishave type 7735 (the 'egg'), 1948.

UV light to combat disease

The Ultrasol was a typical Philips product featuring a beaming lamp at its centre. Ultraviolet light help to combat everyday ailments. The device was the result of research conducted by NatLab staff E.H. Reerink and A. van Wijk on the low-pressure mercury lamp. The Ultrasol was a response to new scientific discoveries. In 1918, a paediatrician based in Berlin had developed a therapy using ultraviolet light to combat rickets that also proved useful in treating anaemia. In the period between the wars, the use of electromagnetic radiation to treat everyday ailments became very popular. Countless high-frequency therapeutic devices and even electric light baths appeared on the market, although their effect was often unclear.

Ultrasol sun lamp, 1930.

Ultraphil

After the war, ultraviolet lamps were increasingly used for cosmetic purposes. Ultraviolet radiation not only helped in combating colds, rickets or lumbago, it also provided a healthy tan that looked athletic, healthy and sophisticated.

Infrared radiation

The Infraphil made a virtue out of the biggest disadvantage of the light bulb: loss of power through heat radiation. The Infraphil's infrared radiation could be directed at a specific part of the body to relieve muscular pain. Even in 2013, the Infraphil is still part of the Philips product range.

Infraphil KL7500, 1960.

Rotating shaver heads

Not all of the brilliant ideas the history of Philips can be attributed to the work of the NatLab. The cassette tape was invented in the Hasselt location, the idea for the Philishave came from engineer Alexandre Horowitz (1904-1982) in the radio factory development department. The rotating shaver heads were his groundbreaking idea. The uninterrupted motion of the rotary blades was significantly more effective than the side-to-side movement on conventional American electric shavers. The rounded head also enabled the user to approach the whiskers from all angles.

Rumour has it that Horowitz came up with his idea when he saw the rotating head of another Philips product – the bicycle dynamo.

Improved Philishave

The Philishave made it big worldwide breakthrough thanks to the double shaver head, which makes shaving faster and did not become as hot as its single-headed predecessor. Work on the development of the double shaver head took place during the war years. However, it could not be marketed until production capacity for the manufacture of the heads was improved.

Philishave 7743, 1951.

And then there were three

After the second head, the third followed at the end of the 1960s. This was a urgently needed response to fierce competition from other manufacturers of electric shavers and even those selling traditional razor blades (and shaving soap) were making important advances. They presented an important innovation: the stainless steel razor blade. A battle of the shavers ensued between wet and dry razors that developed an almost religious tone.

Philishave, 1980.

Epilady

Women became an ever more important target group in the market for electric hair removal.

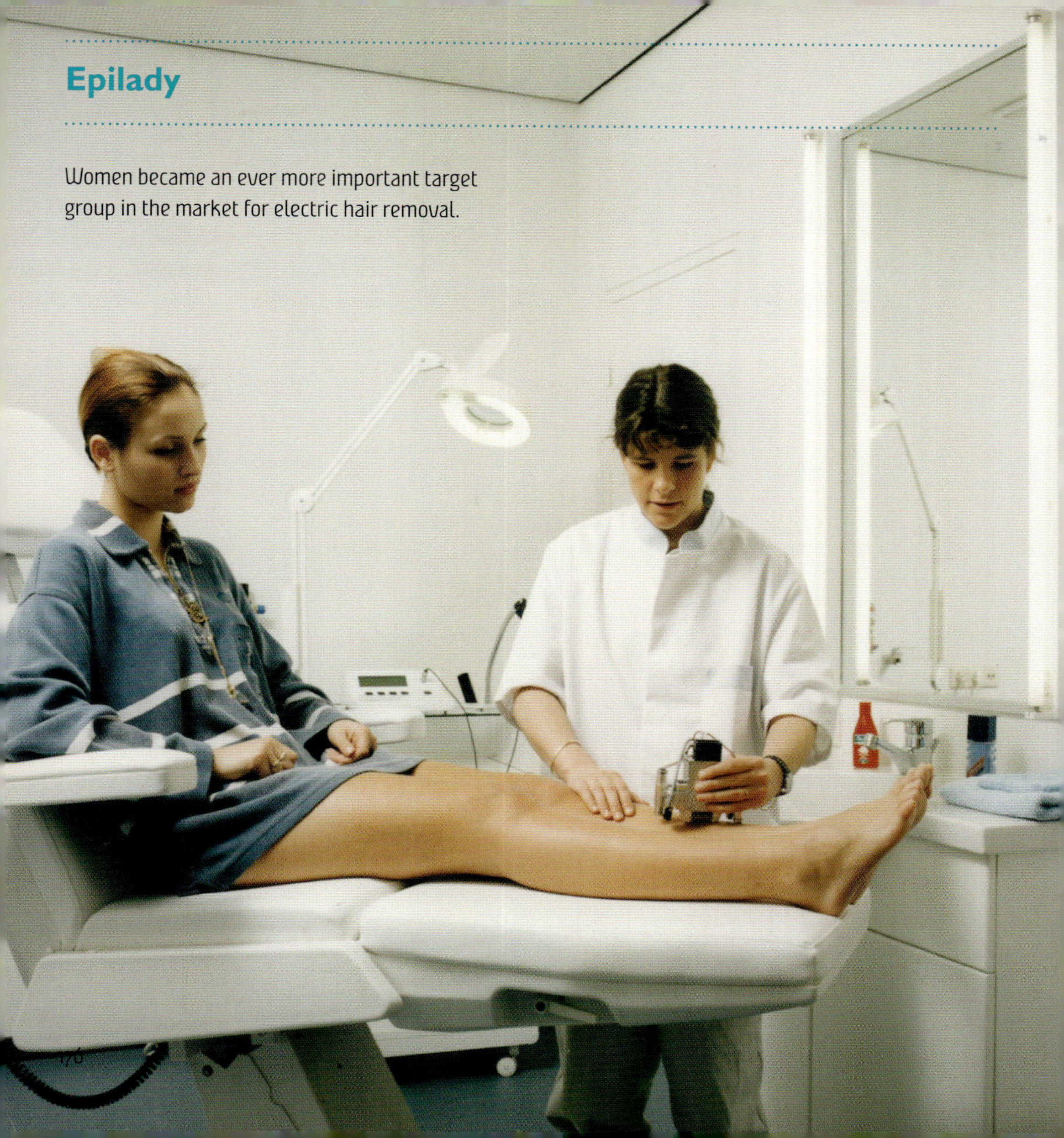

Electric toothbrushes

Other personal care products gradually began to be added to the range.

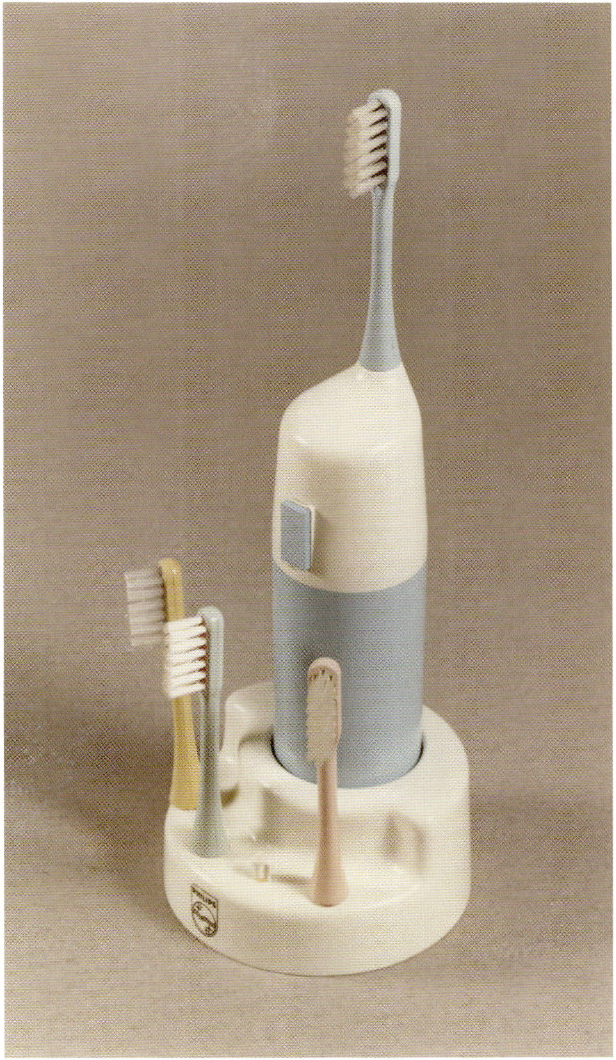

Electric toothbrush HP 5201, 1973.

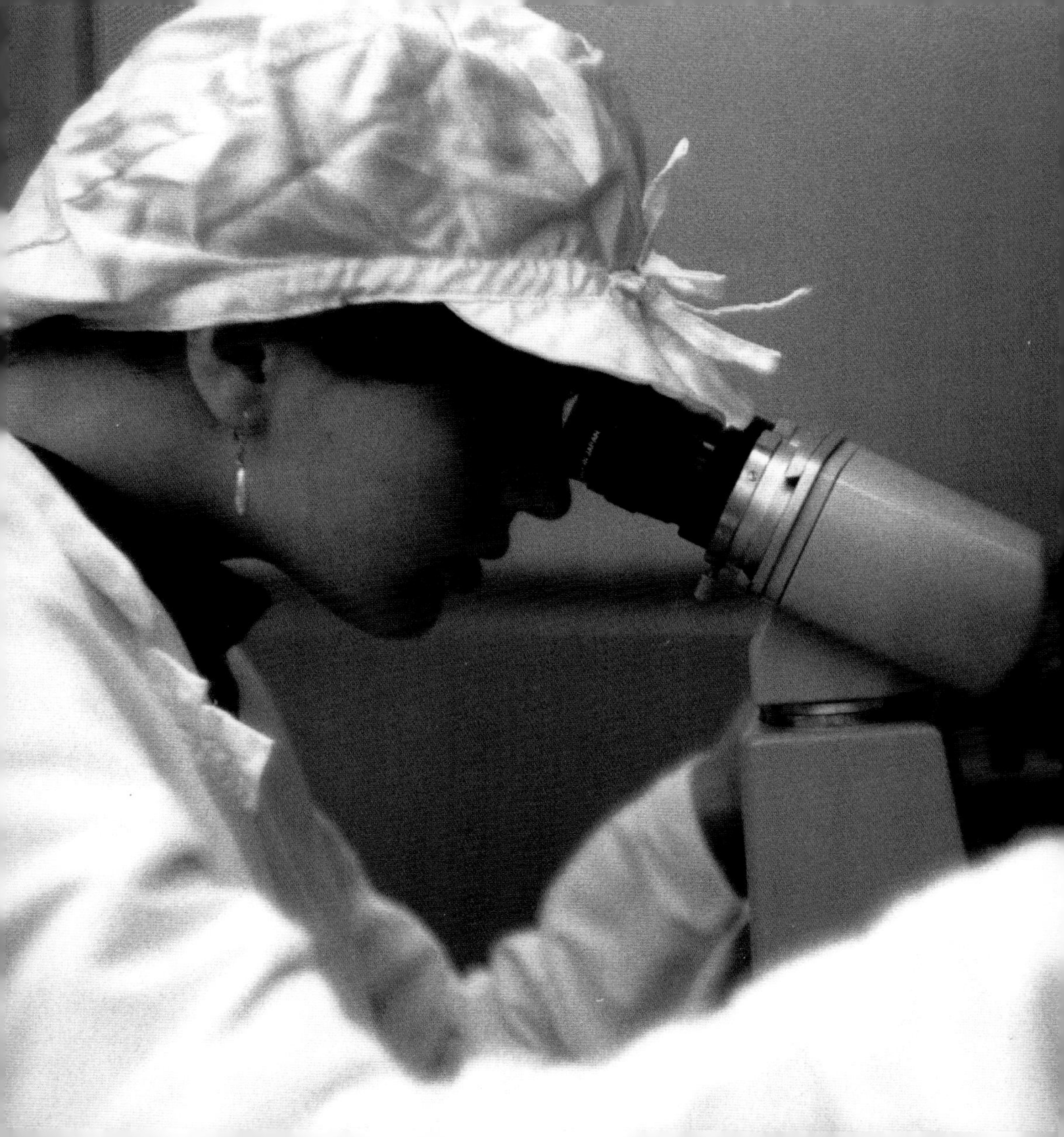

15. The NatLab as seen by Ed van der Elsken

In 1984, the NatLab's head of PR came up with the idea of inviting Ed van der Elsken to do a photo-shoot in the laboratory. Van der Elsken, enfant terrible of Dutch photography, had built up a solid reputation in the 1950s and 1960s as a leading street photographer. As he wandered through world cities, such as Amsterdam, Tokyo and Paris, he would point his camera at colourful, eye-catching individuals. His photograph of three young women crossing the road on Amsterdam's Beethovenstraat won particular acclaim.

In the NatLab, Ed van der Elsken did not photograph abstract science but researchers and clinicians of flesh and blood in their biotope made up of laboratories, conference rooms, workstations, computer prints and chalkboards. At breakneck speed and without a flash, he captured spontaneous shots of the people there. The NatLab management had little control over this self-willed Amsterdammer. In 1989, a selection of black-and-white photographs was published in the booklet entitled *NATLAB*, to mark the 75th anniversary of the laboratory. Together, the photographs present an excellent archive that features a colourful collection of scientists, a race apart within the Philips family, who enjoyed a reputation by virtue of their intelligence but who were also viewed with some suspicion: they were certainly impressive, but what were they actually doing in that secret laboratory?

In 1989, the year in which *NATLAB* was published, the laboratory lost its independent financial position within Philips: from then on the NatLab would need to gather together two-thirds of its budget by securing contracts from the product divisions. It is therefore interesting to take a look at the new mission statement for NatLab formulated in January 1989. It was taken from *NATLAB* and is reproduced in the following series of photographs.

Objective (I)

The objective of Philips Research is to create options for industrial renewal, prepare promising new inventions promptly and transfer them to the product divisions and to build up an excellent position with regard to patents and licences.

Objective (2)

In order to achieve this, an effective international network is necessary with the worlds of science and other industrial research laboratories.

This requires a solid contribution to science by Philips Research itself.

Our research must be at the cutting edge, which means our work must be outstanding. Less than that is not good enough.

Other activities (1)

The NatLab aims to work together with the other research laboratories as the objective technological conscience of Philips. Research that is organised centrally prevents fragmentation of knowledge and expertise and promotes synergy.

Other activities (2)

The NatLab is a source of knowledge and talent for Philips. A NatLab success will only become a real success if it results in a success for Philips.

Style of working (I)

The NatLab has a flexible, rather informal organisation, with open communication in all directions in order to achieve an effective balance between the individuality of the researchers and the coherence of the laboratory as a unit. Researchers must have the space to develop initiatives within their own area for the benefit of Philips.

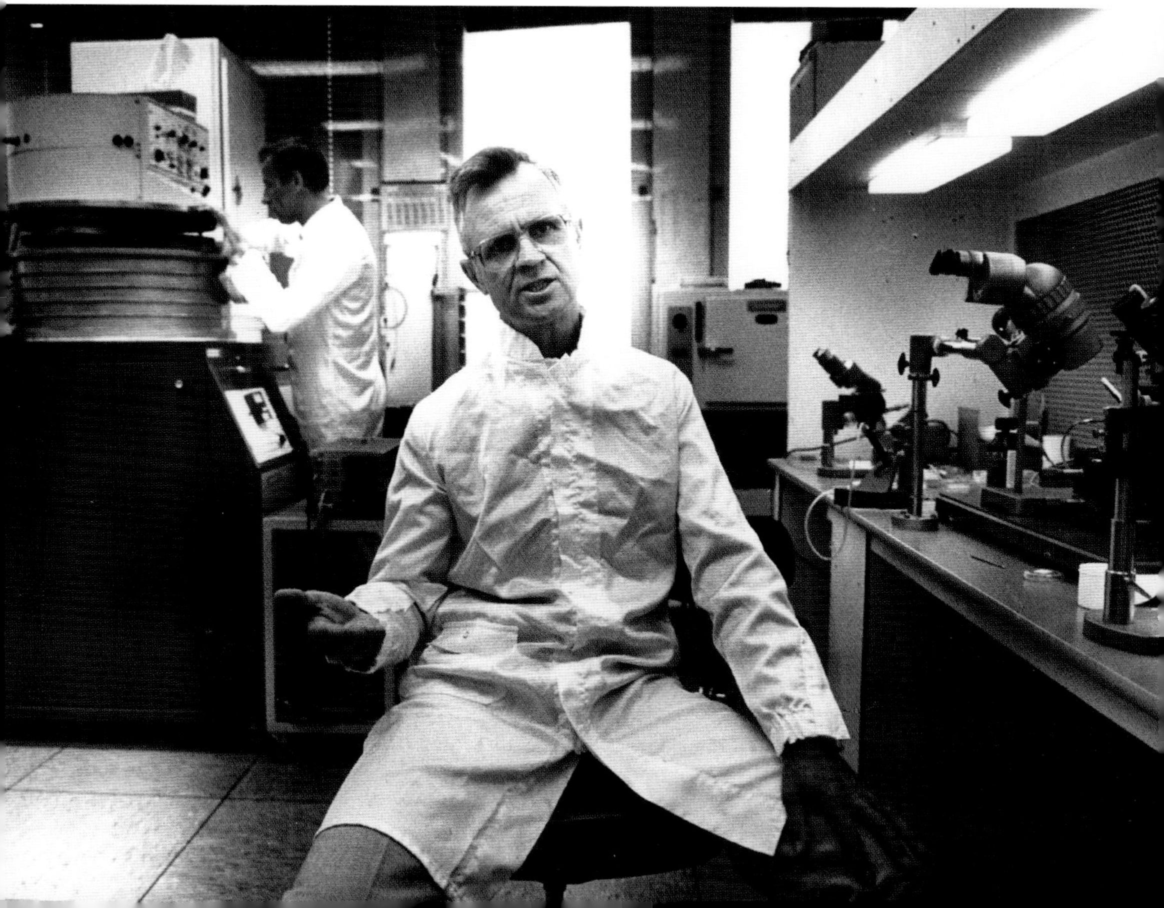

Style of working (2)

The atmosphere in the laboratory is characterised by honesty, collegiality and the sharing of success.

Style of working (3)

Achieving the goals set within the research programme always takes priority and anything that does not contribute to it is of subordinate interest.

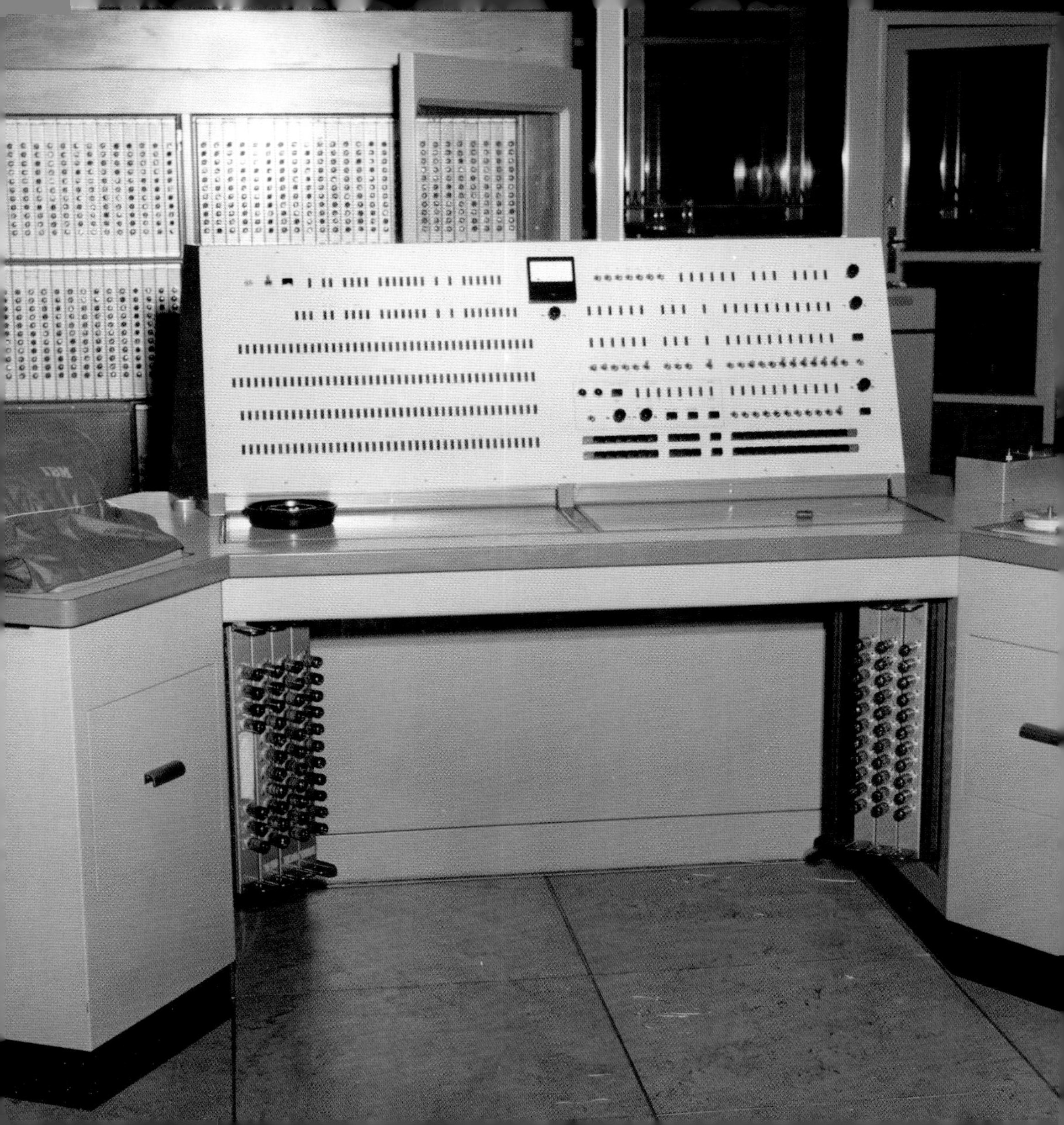

16. Philips digital

For decades, electrical appliances contained tubes to convert alternating current into direct current and amplify it. After the war, semiconductor technology was developed, and would at breakneck speed become the driving force behind the digital revolution of the last decades of the 20th century (and thereafter). An important milestone in this process was the invention of the transistor in the Bell Labs run by American telephone company AT&T: one of the most important breakthroughs ever achieved in electrical engineering. Philips quickly joined the race and earned itself a good market position.

Initially, Philips ran the risk of missing the boat in the field of integrated circuits (transistors and resistors connected together on a thin sheet of silicon). Starting in 1961, American companies Fairchild Semiconductors and Texas Instruments began to market solid-state integrated circuits (ICs or chips). At that time, only a small group of researchers at the NatLab were working on this subject and were using germanium as their basic material rather than silicon. While the company feverishly attempted to keep pace with developments, NatLab engineer Kooi invented LOCOS technology, putting Philips at the forefront of IC developments in a flash.

As for computers, the story was not one of great success. In 1951, NatLab director Rinia believed that these 'thinking machines' were unlikely to be successful. Philips decided to limit its activities to the supplying of components. Despite this, the NatLab developed PETER (Philips Experimentele Tweetalige Elektronische Rekenmachine, 1958) and PASCAL (Philips Akelig Snelle CALculator, 1960). But by the time the Philips Computer Industry division was established in 1963 (with its base in Apeldoorn) and five years later was producing its own computers, it was already too late. It was impossible to catch up with the all-powerful IBM. The production of computers would bring little success for Philips. The company was always slightly behind the state of the art and incurred losses amounting to billions of Dutch guilders.

PASCAL computer, built for the company's own calculations, 1960.

Television transistor

In the first half of the 1950s, Philips, followed at some distance by Siemens, was the only European company to play a role of any importance in the semiconductor industry dominated by American companies. In 1957, the NatLab developed what was known as a base-push-out transistor. This germanium transistor was capable of handling higher frequencies than conventional transistors at that time. This enabled them to be used in television. This success also had a downside: it meant that the company focused much less on silicon as a potential alternative for germanium.

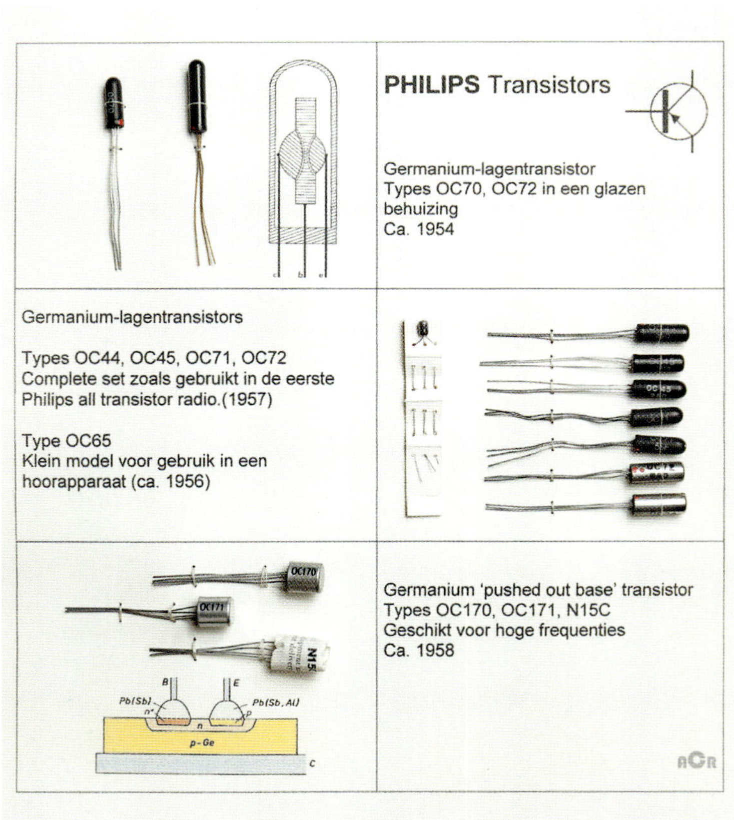

Philips germanium transistors.

LOCOS

Together with the plumbicon, the LOCOS technology was among Philips' most important post-war patents. Without this technology, the production of modern chips with millions of transistors would be unthinkable. LOCOS takes advantage of the fact that it is possible to etch patterns through (localised) oxidation of the silicon. This enables transistors to be insulated from each other in a way that saves space. LOCOS made the manufacture of more compact chips possible along with the production of new types of ICs.

LOCOS was invented in 1966 by Else Kooi, who had begun work in the NatLab in 1956 to achieve the shift from germanium to silicon as the basic material for ICs.

Else Kooi.

Electrologica

In order to make it easier to enter the computer market, Philips acquired the company Electrologica. This Dutch computer manufacturer emerged as a result of an alliance between insurance company Nillmij and the Mathematics Centre at the University of Amsterdam, where mathematicians had been working on the development of their own computers since the 1940s. With its X1 – one of the first machines fully equipped with transistors – Electrologica was launching a state-of-the-art computer onto the market.

The Electrologica X1 is commissioned.

The P-1000 computer

In 1969, Philips started the production of its own series of computers, P-1000. This included three types of highly advanced mid-range mainframe computers. After a year and a half, only 41 have been sold, 31 of them within the company itself. The Philips sales organisations were not sufficiently equipped to market the machine, but the main cause was the market domination by IBM. Philips was too far behind to poach custom from the computer giant. The fact that this fate befell the whole of the European computer industry was little comfort.

This P-2000 personal computer was placed on the market in 1981.

The Videopac G 7000

As well as mainframes, Philips also marketed a complete range of different types of computers: bank terminals, mini-computers, office computers, word processors and games computers. The success of the Videopac G 7000 is proof that not all of the company's computer activities were doomed to failure.

NXP

Almost every car currently being manufactured contains NXP semiconductor technology. This company, based in Nijmegen, came about in 2006 when the Philips Semiconductors division gained independence. NXP manufactures a wide range of semiconductors used in all kinds of areas.

ASML wafer steppers

Wafer steppers are the machines that use lasers to place transistor patterns on a thin sheet of silicon (wafer), forming the basis for a chip. The Dutch company ASML builds wafer steppers. ASML is one of the key drivers behind Moore's law, which predicts that the number of transistors on integrated circuits will double every two years (making computers ever more powerful). As wafer steppers and related equipment become ever more advanced, it becomes possible to engrave increasing numbers of circuits on silicon wafers, thereby continually increasing storage capacity. ASML started life in 1984 as a joint-venture between Philips and ASM International. The aim was to market Philips' stepper Sira III. Since then, ASML has grown to become the world market leader in chip machines. There is a very high likelihood that the chips in your (increasingly fast) computer or telephone were produced using a machine from ASML.

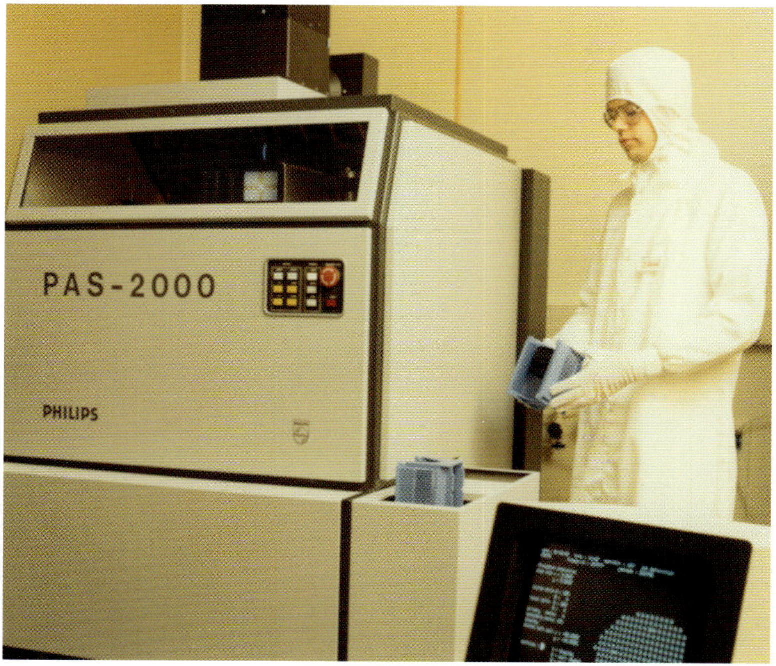

First wafer stepper, 1981.

Videowriter

The Videowriter from 1985 was a word processor with a characteristic amber-coloured monitor and floppy disks on which to store the texts.

PHILIPS

17. Philips Research abroad

Philips operates worldwide, and Philips Research is spread across six international locations, with Eindhoven serving as its headquarters. Each of these locations has its own specialisms and fulfils a range of different functions at local level. Despite this, there is now much more coordination than there was in the past. Currently, the amount of research conducted abroad is growing relative to that in Eindhoven. However, the overall amount of research conducted has been reduced significantly in the last quarter of a century, reflecting the disposal of whole corporate divisions such as microscopy, semiconductors and parts of consumer electronics. The current research locations, with the number of staff in brackets are: Bangalore (30), Briarcliff (125), Cambridge (35), Eindhoven (1500), Hamburg (100) and Shanghai (110). Some of the research laboratories abroad, including the one in Brussels, have been closed, but Philips Research is also about to open a new facility in Brazil. The Philips Lumiblade Creative Lab, located in Aachen, works on the development of OLEDs.

In Briarcliff (New York), the research is concentrated on *Lighting and Healthcare*. Until recently, Philips owned the nearby SuperPower, an innovative company that develops superconducting coils that need reduced cooling compared with those used in current MRI scanners (with liquid nitrogen instead of liquid helium). Intermagnetics, which develops and builds MRI scanners and is also located nearby was acquired by Philips in 2006. The laboratory in Hamburg also conducts research into imaging technologies such as MRI.

The research facilities in the Far East are relatively young. In Bangalore, the heart of Silicon Valley in India, local emerging markets determine the choice of research subjects: photovoltaic solar cells, neonatal care, cervical cancer screening. The research conducted in Shanghai is also predominantly consumer-led.

Research into virtual reality, Redhill (UK), 1997.

Coils in Hamburg

In Hamburg, research is being conducted into gradient coils. In practice, an MRI scanner consists of several coils. The outermost coil creates a powerful magnetic field. The patient lies in the cylindrical opening – for very overweight patients and those with claustrophobia, open MRI systems are now available. The large magnet makes use of superconductivity, which means a cooling system is required. In order to reduce the magnetic field outside the scanner, shield coils are installed in which the current flows in reverse. An additional gradient coil enables the strength of the field in the patient to be adjusted locally so that the location of the signal can be precisely determined. Detectors capture this signal and the computer converts all of this into an image.

ICs in Briarcliff

Research into the manufacture of ICs in the laboratory in Briarcliff, 1986. The location, near New York, was chosen strategically in order to link in as much as possible with the innovative ecosystem in the Boston-Washington DC corridor, where numerous companies involved in medicines, healthcare and biomedical technology are based. There are also many government-funded institutes working in these areas. The American Philips research facility focuses primarily on *Healthcare and Lighting*.

Fingerprints in Redhill

Shot of research into a sensor for taking fingerprints, Redhill, 1997. The British Philips Research facility was originally based in Redhill, at the Mullard Research Laboratories site. It has been based in Cambridge since 2008.

Sheets of light in Aachen

Discussion in front of a whiteboard in Aachen, 2000. Philips in Aachen was the most important German location and started life as a light bulb factory in 1934. A glass factory was built in 1948. There was also a cathode ray tube factory. Both factories have since closed, making Hamburg the largest location in Germany. However, Aachen remains the world production centre for car lamps and is currently the centre for OLED research. OLEDs are organic LEDs (light emitting diodes) that enable large surfaces of light to be projected.

Taipei

Repairs to a STB5660-box in the research laboratory in Taipei (Taiwan), 1998. This facility has since closed in favour of the one in Shanghai.

Shanghai and Asian cuisine

Laboratory equipment for research into high-speed CD+RW recording, Shanghai. Philips Research in Shanghai is consumer-driven. The laboratory focuses on *Consumer Lifestyle* areas such as Asian cuisine, care for mother and child and water and air purification.

The chips of Bangalore

Research into Nexperia chips in Bangalore. Nexperia chips are the nerve centre of various consumer appliances, including mobile telephones and TVs.

Workshop in Cambridge

From its research laboratory in Cambridge, Philips works together with other innovative organisations. One example is the Microfluids Consortium, which aims to use extremely small-volume fluid streams for medical purposes. The photograph shows a workshop run by this consortium.

Briarcliff and the heart

Researchers in Briarcliff use the 'Allura FD10 X-ray fluoroscopy system' to assist and lead research into heart disease. The system enables an efficient workflow whilst keeping X-ray doses low.

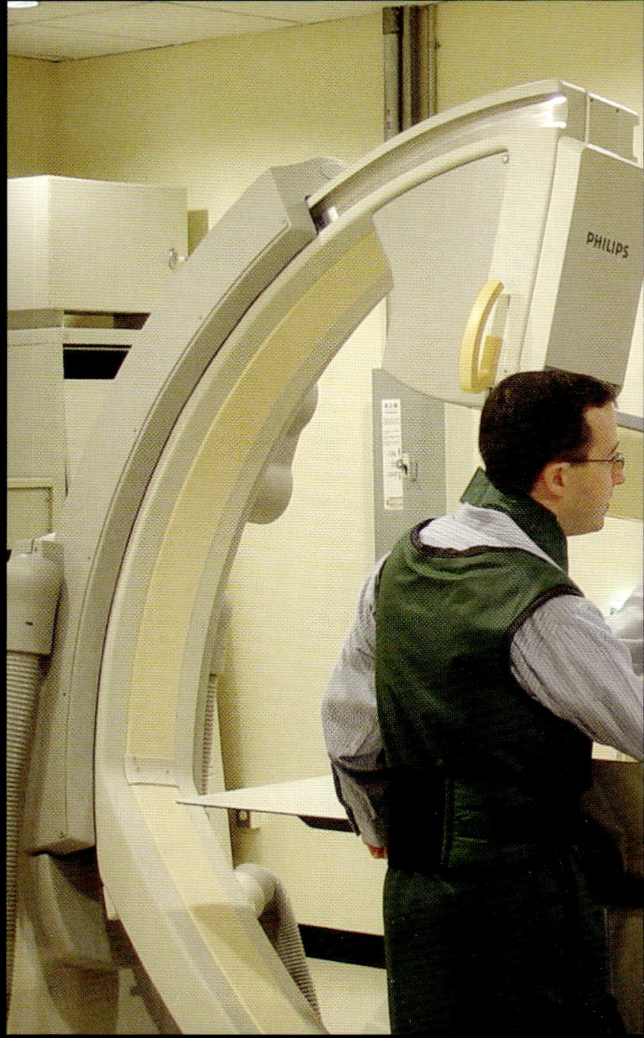

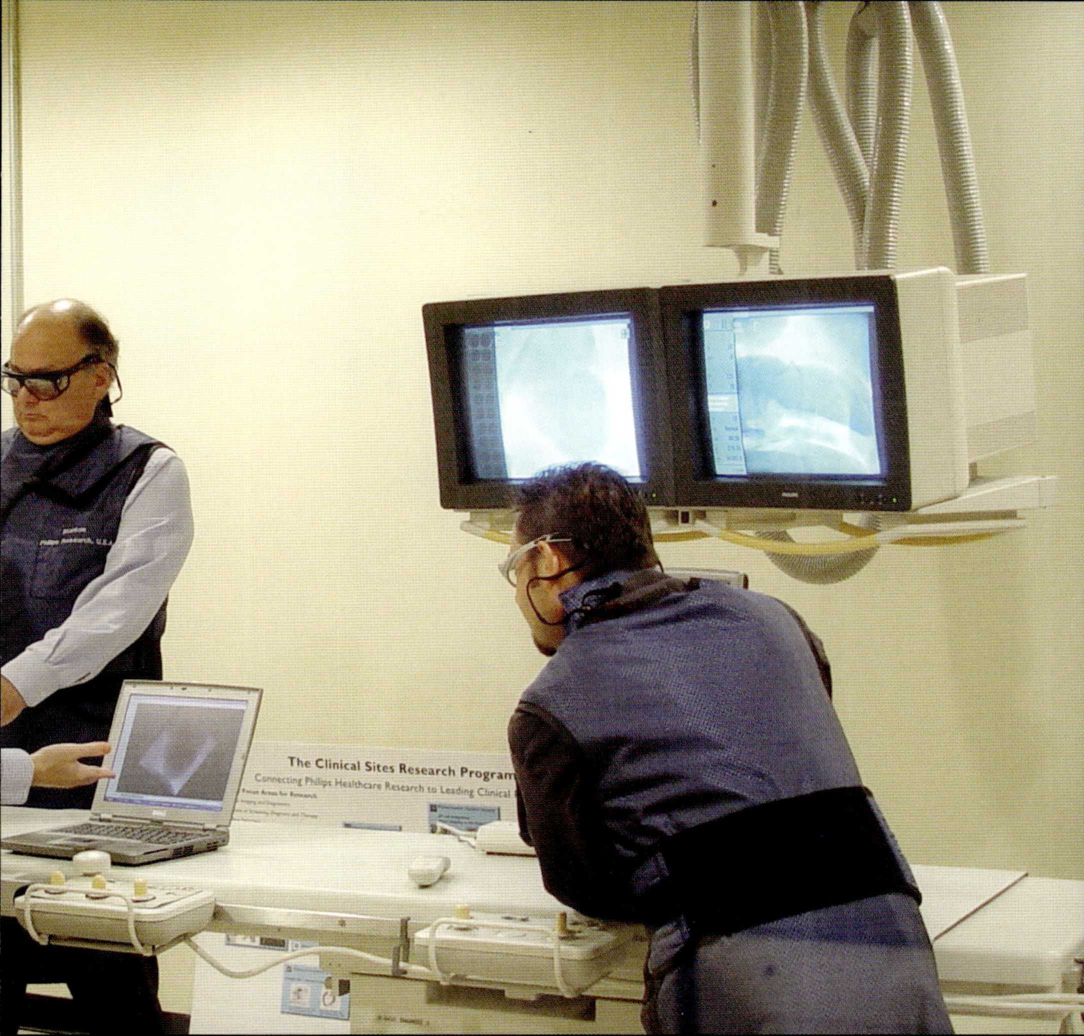
The Clinical Sites Research Program
Connecting Philips Healthcare Research to Leading Clinical

PHILIPS
TOCH BETER
Prelude
Rondo

18. Advertising and design

In late 1924, Louis Kalff, son of the editor-in-chief of the Dutch newspaper *Algemeen Handelsblad*, sent a challenging letter to Anton Philips. Kalff, who had studied architecture in Delft after attending art school in Amsterdam (now the Rietveld Academie) informed the Philips boss that the company's advertising was old-fashioned and unworthy of a major international company. He himself would approach it completely differently. Anton Philips was impressed by Kalff's ideas and appointed the newly-qualified architect as head of its Commercial and Artistic Propaganda department, the precursor to Philips Design. Kalff was assisted in this by his friendship with Frans Otten, Anton Philips' future son-in-law (and, from 1939, his successor).

Before the arrival of Kalff, Philips' advertising was a mishmash of different styles. Each designer used their own font and logo. On his appointment, Kalff immediately began to modernise and, in 1925, when the Philips radio began to take off, he introduced matching stars and waves for the B406l radio lamp packaging. The word PHILIPS (in upper case) also originates from the 1920s and the famous Philips shield dates from 1938. Both versions of the Philips brand, including the precisely-defined contexts in which designers had to use them, were recorded in 1973 in the *First House Style Manual*.

It was during this period that Computer Aided Design first began to be used. Rotating three-dimensional models on the screen make the construction of prototypes unnecessary in many cases and the designer is free to try out endless variations. Sustainable design is the modern buzzword: it means more than green, technological or environmentally-friendly. Sustainable design is also about social responsibility and economic viability. In other words, the balance between 'Planet, People and Profit'.

Louis Kalff

Louis Kalff (1897-1976) was the first person within Philips to approach design professionally.

He grew up in Amsterdam surrounded by culture: his father was head of the art department at the *Algemeen Handelsblad* (and later editor-in-chief). Writers, painters, musicians and other artists were regular visitors to his home. Kalff was the architect behind the design of some impressive Philips buildings, including the Dr. A.F. Philips Sterrenwacht and the Evoluon, both in Eindhoven.

First advertising poster

The first poster that Louis Kalff designed for Philips in 1925 was an advertising poster for Duplo adjustable car lamps.

Waves and stars

The stars and waves in the Philips emblem were introduced in 1925 by accident. Kalff had no idea how radio worked, asked someone about it and was told it was related to waves in the air that transmitted the sound. Kalff therefore designed packaging for the mini-watt vacuum tube consisting of four-pointed yellow stars on a purple background with a band of red waves underneath.

The Philips shield

The famous Philips shield was an outstanding success. When it was launched, Anton Philips was extremely enthusiastic and had enamel badges made featuring the Philips shield that guards wore on their caps and that were distributed en masse at trade fairs.

The Philishave since 1939

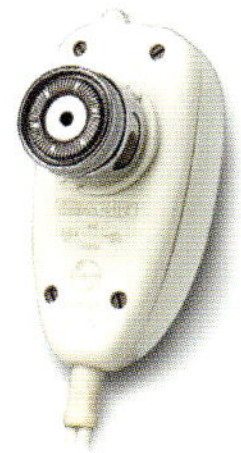

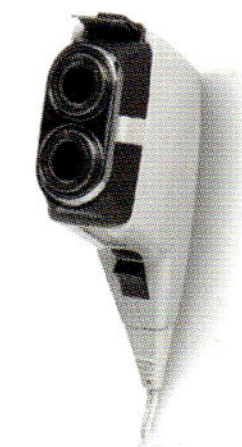

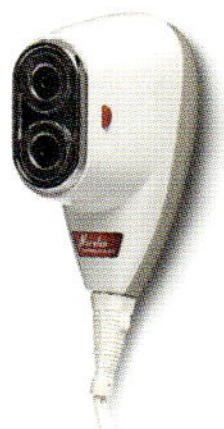

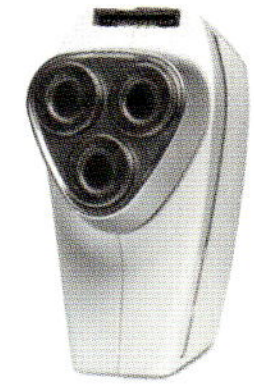

One of the most successful Philips products ever was the electric dry shaver, the Philishave.

The picture shows the shaver's development and design since its introduction in 1939.

A personalised kitchen

In 1994, Stefano Marzano (Varese, 1950), then Head of Corporate Industrial Design at Philips, entered into an alliance with Italian firm Alessi for electric kitchen equipment. The Philips-Alessi range included four products: a toaster, a fruit juicer, a coffee machine and a kettle. The rounded shapes and pastel colours had not been seen in kitchens before and set a trend for the rest of the decade. From then on, kitchens revealed something about their owners' personality.

PHILIPS
ALESSI
PHILIPS

The cheerful hand blender

The Billy hand blender is as cheerful as it gets. Introduced at the start of this century, sales exceeded all expectations. Billy was not only effective, it also had character and was 'chic, sophisticated and sexy'. Consumers were bowled over by the design. Philips had learnt a valuable lesson: who dares wins.

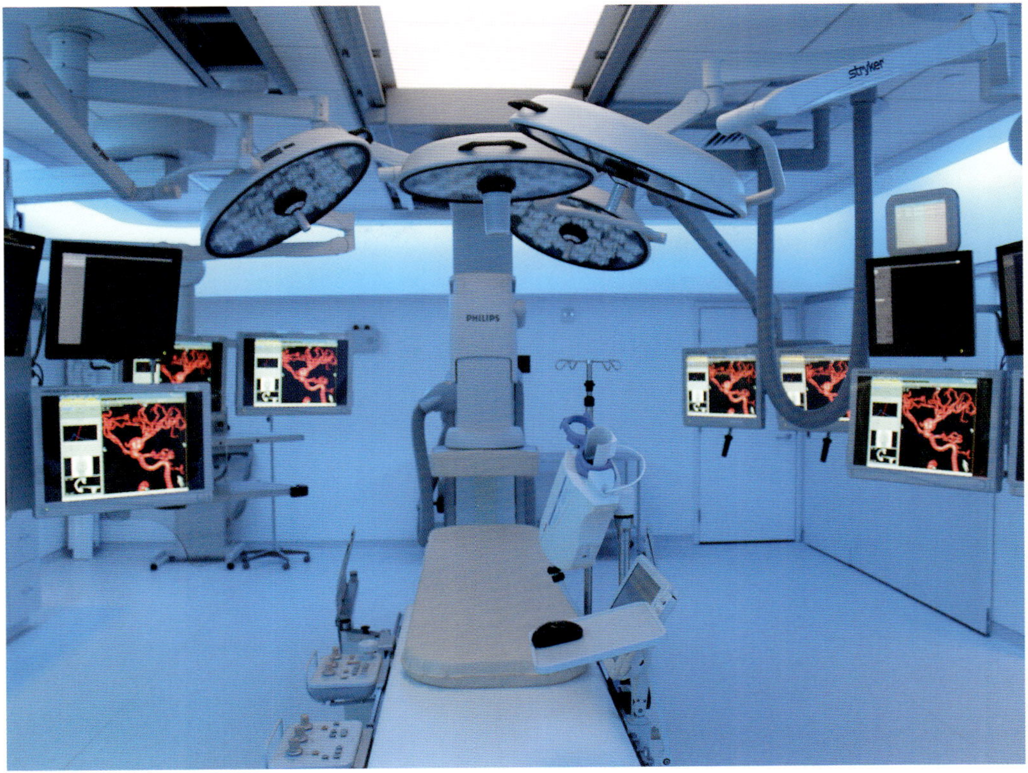

Ambient Experience in the operating theatre

Philips designs complete hospital facilities. The picture shows an award-winning design from 2013 of the operating theatre equipped with Ambient Experience, creating a calming environment for the patient.

In the new Rijksmuseum, the lighting has been supplied by Philips.

19. Shining a new light

On 27 November 2012, the Empire State Building was suddenly bathed in a sea of coloured light. Philips was using the iconic building to demonstrate the power of modern LED technology. At nine in the morning, singer Alicia Keys touched a button to begin a spectacle of light using LED lighting. At precisely the same time, the radio was broadcasting her hit single 'Empire State of Mind'. Previously illuminated using static lights in just ten colours, the building's new lighting incorporated as many as 16 million, in all imaginable combinations, with patterns and effects that linger over the building, jump around, flicker, merge and explode. Magic created by light.

A few months later, on 13 April 2013, Dutch Queen Beatrix opened the new Rijksmuseum in Amsterdam after a decade of renovations. There too, the building and works of art were illuminated by LED lights, developed, produced and installed by Philips. The lighting plan incorporated as many as three-quarters of a million LEDs. These included 3,800 LED spotlights, more than 1.8 km of LED lighting for the ceiling and an advanced operating system that museum staff operate remotely using a portable application.

Philips takes a completely different perspective on light than it did just a century ago. Now, everything revolves around sustainability. Almost 20% of the world's electricity consumption is used on lighting. As the world's population and its need for energy grows, the challenge is to develop creative and energy-efficient solutions, with LED lights taking centre stage. One new development is the integration of light within clothing and carpets. Or intelligent light that is capable of making targeted content appear almost by magic on a nearby smartphone or tablet. Or 'Luminous Surfaces' that interact elegantly and playfully with people standing in front of them.

The impact that light has on people and animals has now also become a subject for research. Knowledge about the influence of light on our health and well-being is extremely important for the development of new products.

Bay Bridge

In March 2013, the western side of San Francisco's Bay Bridge was transformed into a light sculpture made up of 6 km of LED lighting. Installed by Philips Color Kinetics, it consumes just $ 4.25 worth of energy per hour – generated by solar panels. The 25,000 LED nodes on the bridge each have 255 different intensity settings and countless colours. For two whole years, an orchestra of light, designed by Leo Villareal and featuring a lot of playful geometry, is set to impress the residents of San Francisco. From the bridge itself, you can see nothing.

Illuminating fashion

LEDs are so small and flexible that fashion designers have been eager to use them in their creations. This Bubelle dress from 2007 has two layers. The innermost layer features biometric sensors that can detect emotions and the outer layer of the dress displays these emotions using LED light.

The organic LED

At the Philips Innovation Experience 2011, held to mark the company's 120th anniversary in the Evoluon, there were demonstrations of OLED. This is an LED made from organic materials. OLED does not provide bright targeted light, like LED does, but radiates a diffuse light across a whole surface. By controlling each surface separately, it is possible to create dynamic images. OLEDS are used for display or as a source of light.

A light button on the smartphone

Hue lighting is an innovation that enables you to adjust the colour and intensity of the lighting in your living room using an app on your smartphone.

Hue is made up of LED lights with standard fittings connected to the web by Wi-Fi.

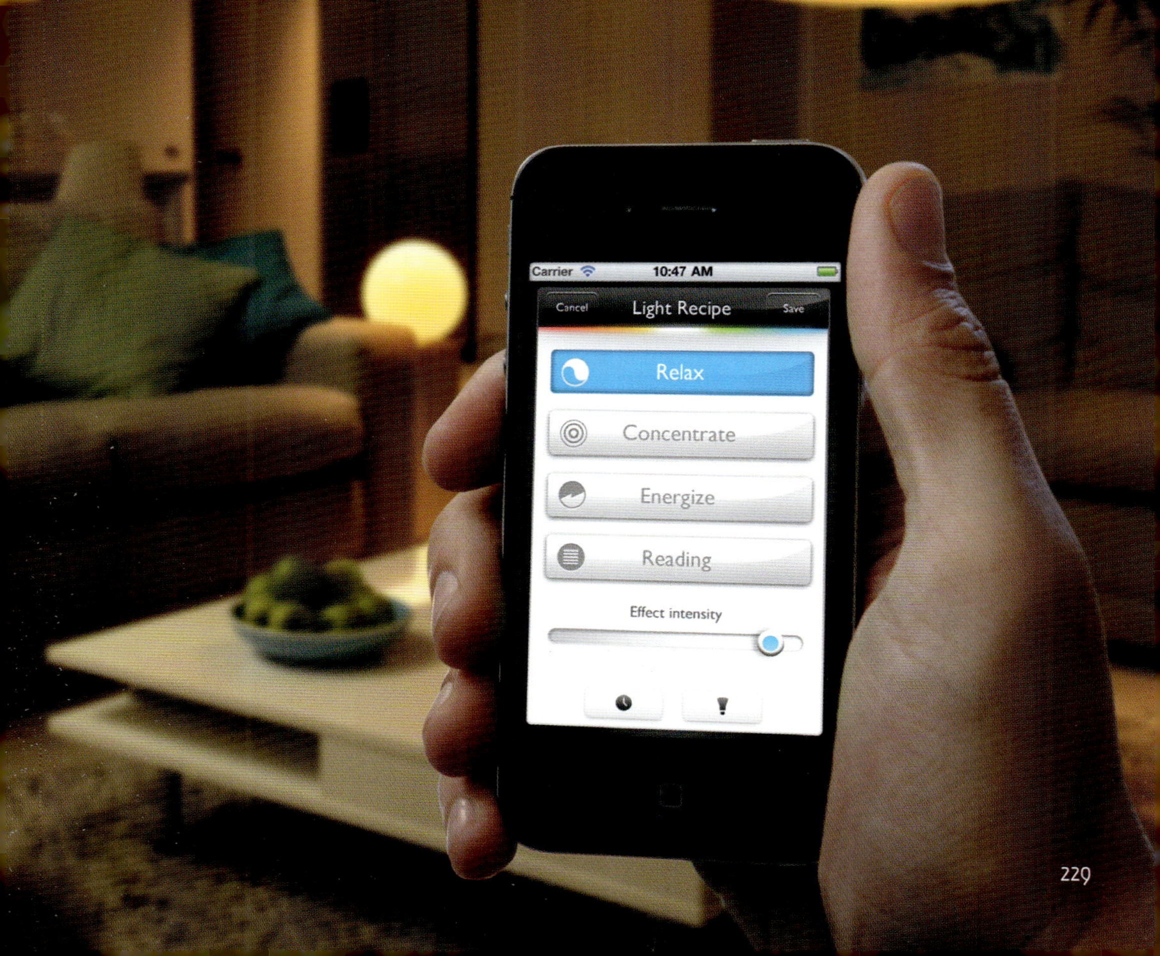

Light enables active paint

The City of the Hague is conducting a pilot using air purification paint in its Koningstunnel. Ultraviolet light from Philips fluorescent tubes is shone on a special exterior paint containing ultrafine titanium dioxide. The ultraviolet light activates the paint's air purification effect as a result of which nitrogen oxides from car emissions are broken down. The result is improved air quality.

Solar Power

Philips Community Light Centers are special sites covering approximately a thousand square metres illuminated by efficient LED lights linked to solar cells and batteries. In developing countries, where there is often no electricity network, this is a major step forward.

Bird lighting

In order to prevent migratory birds colliding with oil platforms, Philips has installed the so-called Bird Light as part of a pilot on a Dutch oil platform run by the Dutch oil company NAM near Vlieland. Bird Light excludes the red component from the spectrum, as a result of which birds become less confused than they would in normal light.

Replacement for the fluorescent tube

Philips Research has developed a TLED prototype. T stands for 'tubular' or 'tube', and originates from tl: 'tube luminescent'. This future replacement for the fluorescent tube produces 200 lumen per watt of warm, white light, making it twice as efficient as the conventional fluorescent tube. Scheduled for market launch in 2015, TLED has huge potential for saving energy.

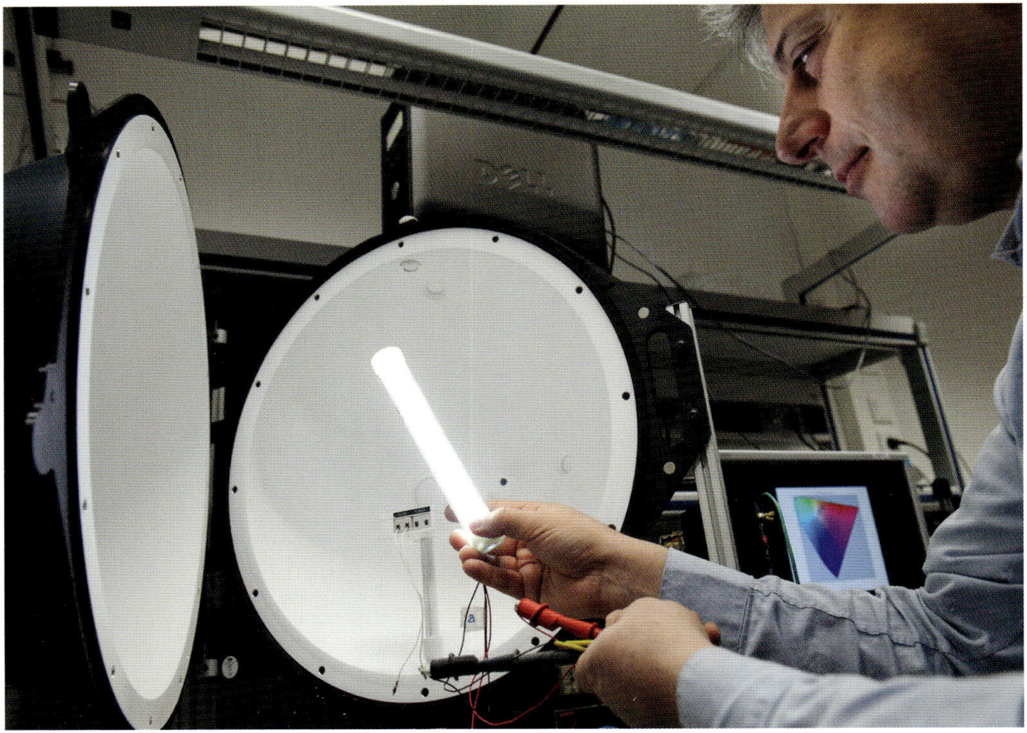

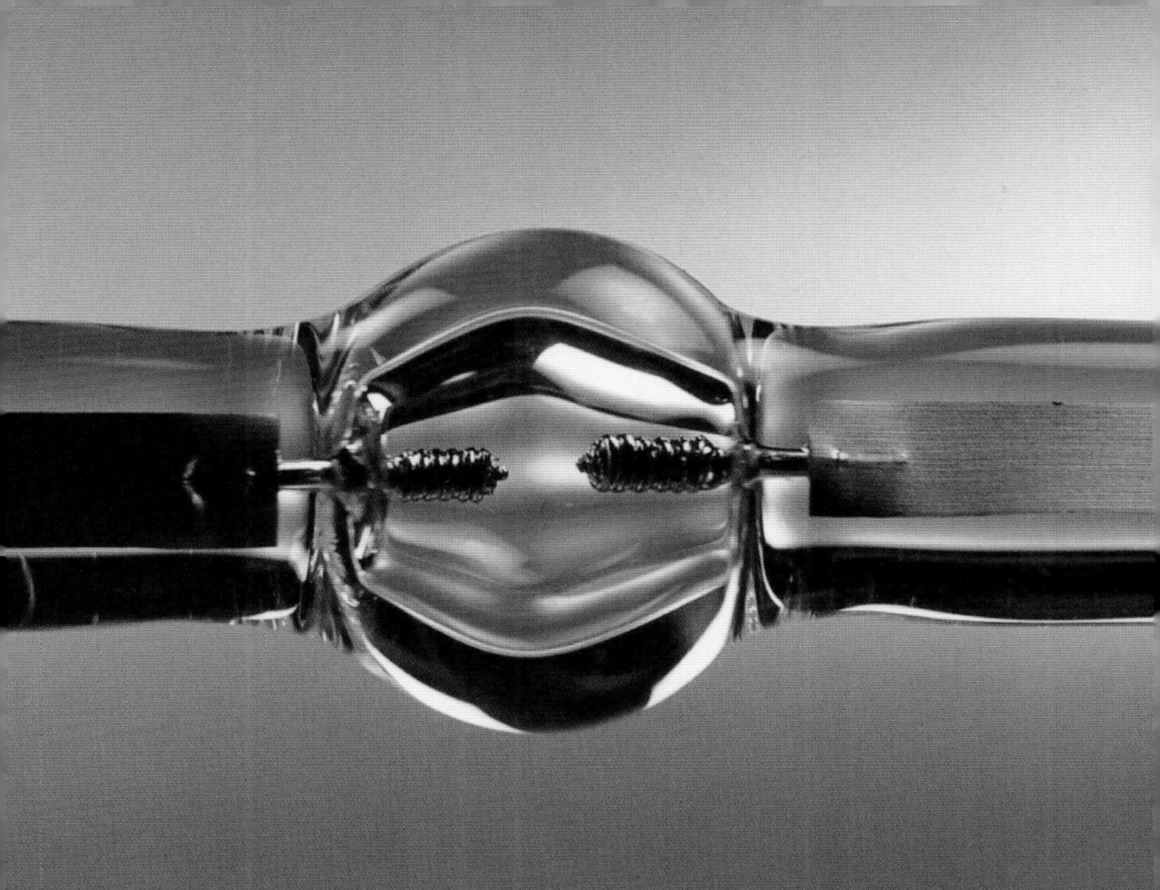

Putting the sun in the shade

A UHP lamp (Ultra High Performance) shines brighter than the sun. This, combined with a lifetime lasting 10,000 hours, makes it perfect for projection.

20. An eye for technology and the patient

Since Philips started to repair broken X-ray tubes during the First World War, Philips Research has been active in medical technology. In the early days, the iron lung and hearing aids were obvious examples, but imaging technologies such as MRI are the main focus today.

Philips Healthcare aims to respond to trends in modern healthcare. The world population continues to increase and is also ageing. People with chronic diseases now live longer and medical costs are spiralling out of control. Care at home will increasingly replace hospital care. At the same time, people are becoming more aware of the influence of lifestyle on health. In healthcare, the ageing population is an enormous problem that calls for sustainable solutions to prevent the costs becoming uncontrollable.

Philips Healthcare believes that the remedy must come in the form of an integrated approach, with patient and care provider playing a central role. This covers the entire cycle of care, from disease prevention to screening, diagnosis, treatment and after-care, at home or in the hospital. Philips Research is therefore also conducting research into treatment rooms where people feel more comfortable. Another example is the wake-up light inspired by the natural sunrise, as a way of starting the day feeling fitter. It is research with a human dimension.

The MRI scanner

MRI stands for Magnetic Resonance Imaging: powerful magnetic fields make the various tissues in the body visible, and reveal their condition, healthy or otherwise. At its core, the device is made up of several superconducting coils. The first brain scans date back to the 1970s. Philips builds its scanners in Albany (New York) and conducts research to improve the scanner. The location in Hamburg has a 'Tomographic Imaging Group with an MR Front-End Hardware cluster'. In other words, research is conducted into imaging systems, including MRI scanners. These are complicated machines that combine a range of different technologies: high-power electrical engineering, high-frequency electromagnetic waves, magnet technology, signalling technology and signal processing.

Magnetic field

Designing an MRI scanner involves major issues of optimisation. How powerful should the magnetic field be? How large should the volume of the field be that is of sufficient quality to create images? How large should the opening be (in other words how big can the patient be)? By far the most expensive component is the magnet.

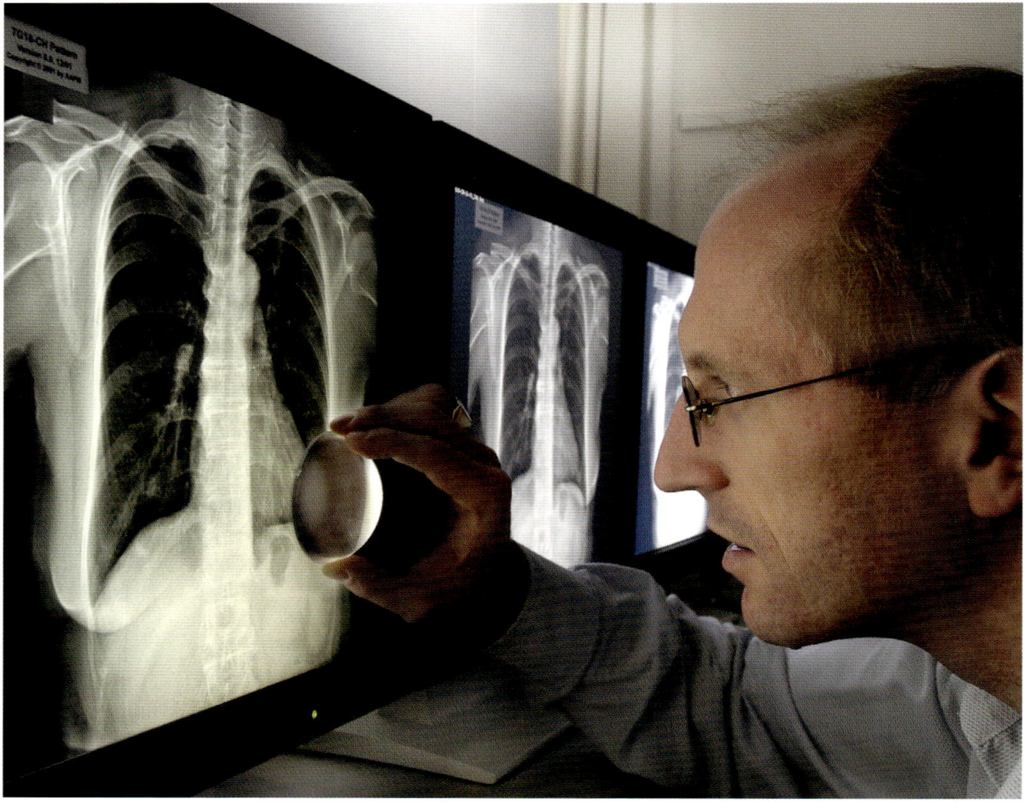

Clear images

Prototype of an LCD screen that enhances the contrast and detail of X-rays. An LCD screen (liquid crystal display) is based, as its name suggests, on liquid crystals.

ECG shirt

Applying the motto, 'prevention is better than cure', flexible electrodes have been sewn into this shirt to record the patient's electrocardiogram. This enables heart failure to be detected at an early stage.

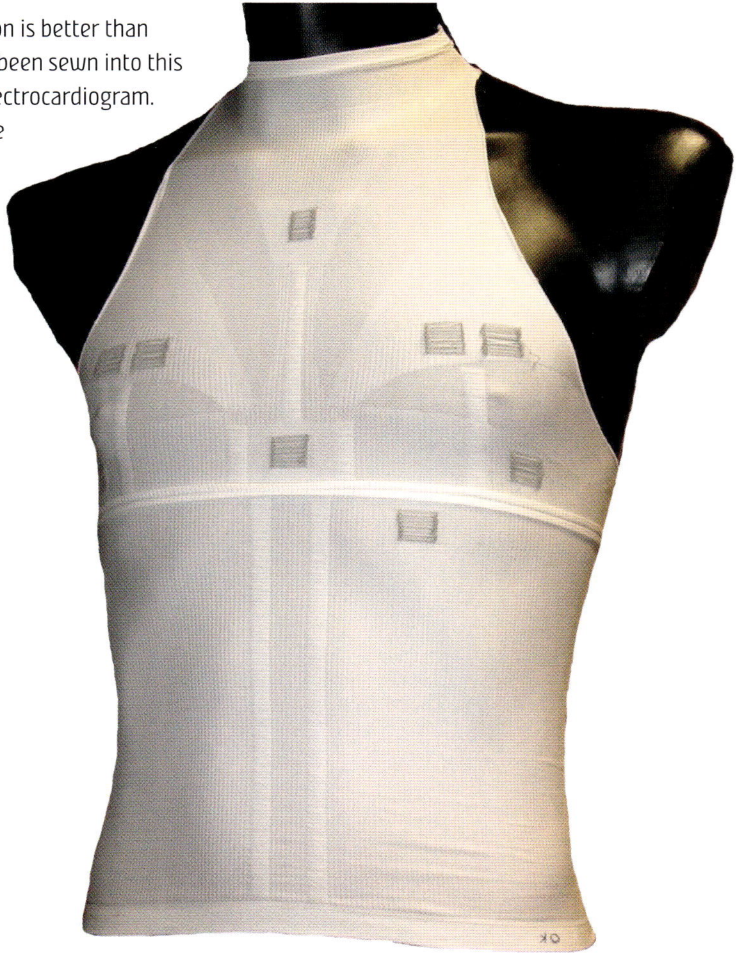

Laboratory readings

A biophysical researcher from Philips Research works on glucose readings for diabetic patients.

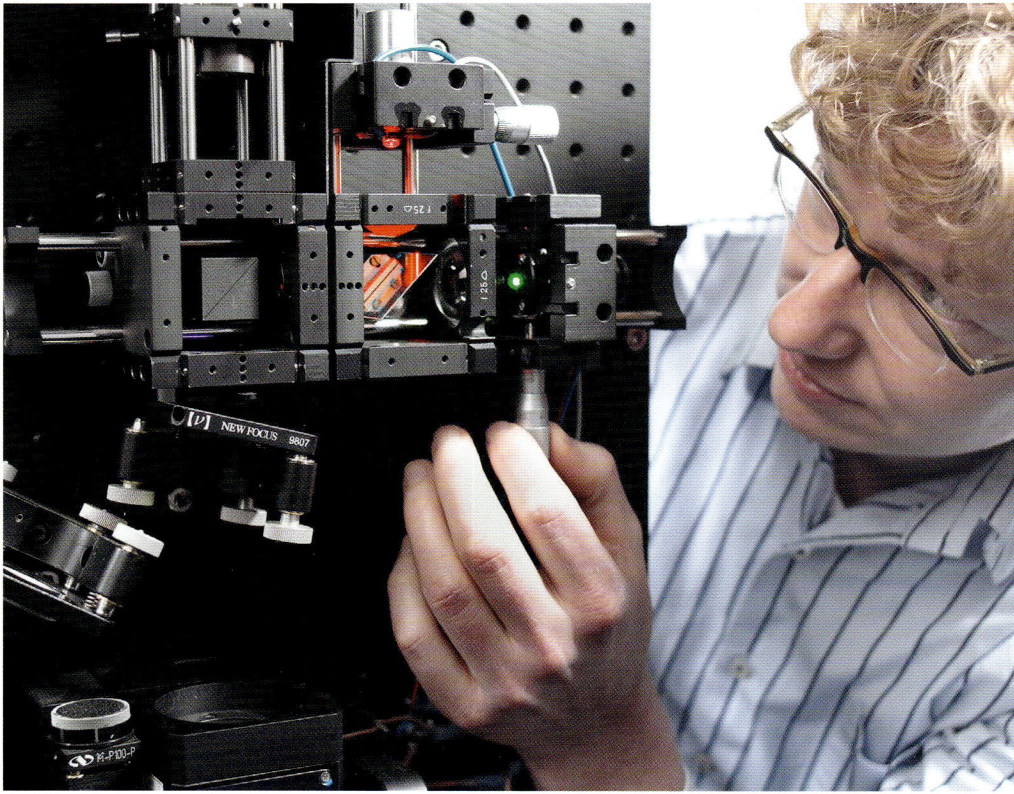

Detailed ultrasound

In August 2013, Philips Healthcare introduced EPIC, a new method for producing ultrasound images. The innovative aspect is nSIGHT, an imaging technology developed by Philips that delivers startlingly detailed images.

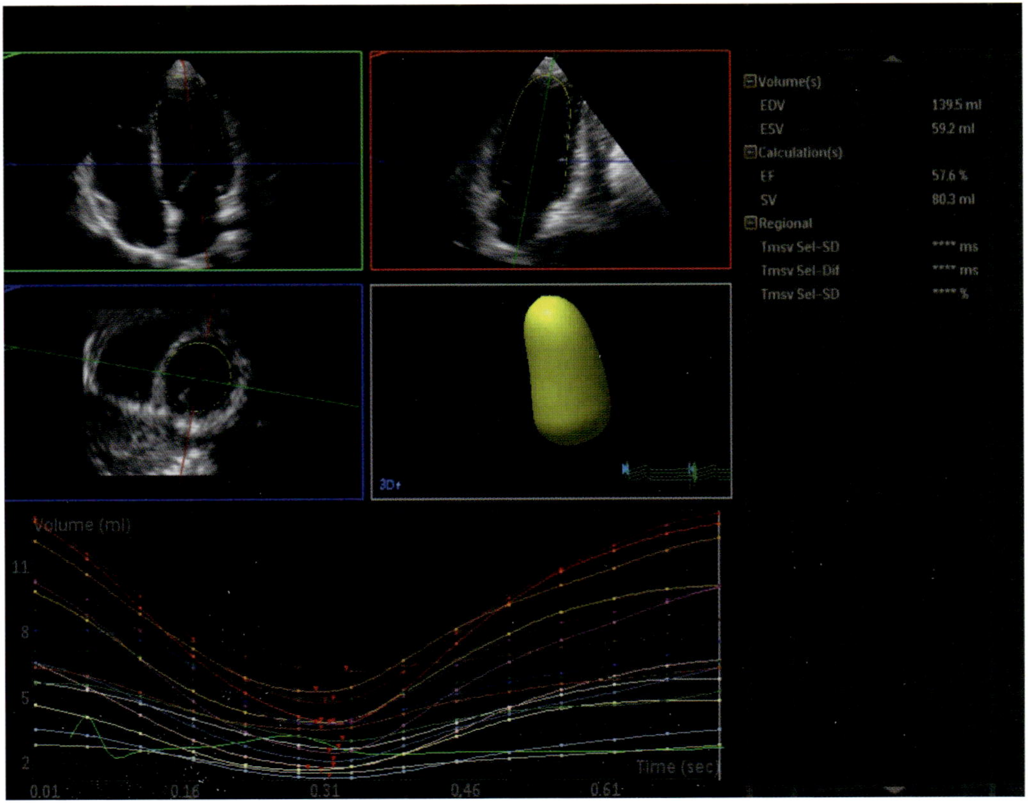

Smart bedding

Biomedical bedding monitors sleep quality by measuring breathing and heart rate in the form of subtle variations in pressure.

Stars on the ceiling

In the Ambient Experience Radiology Suite developed by Philips, cheerful animations appear on the ceiling and walls in order to relax patients who are about to undergo a scan.

Computer Aided Design to combat dementia

The degeneration of the brain that leads to dementia can be diagnosed using a PET scan (positron electron tomography). Philips Research has developed software that can interpret this type of scan automatically. The picture shows a screenshot from the system.

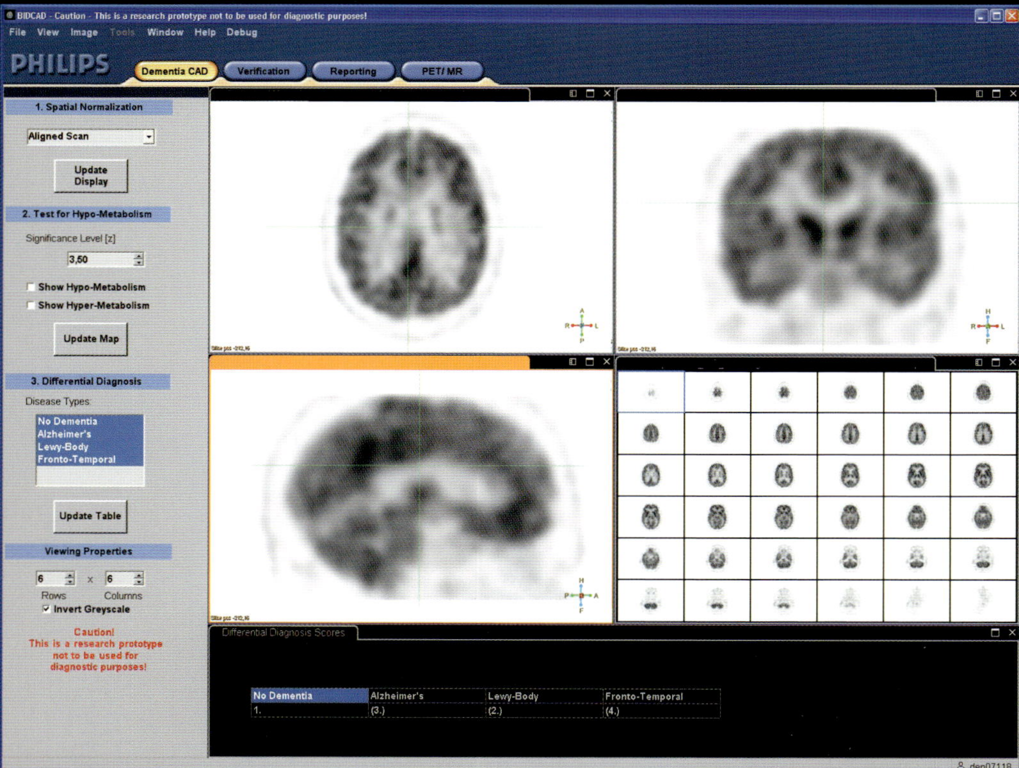

Microbubbles

Microbubbles (extremely tiny droplets of fluid) are used in imaging technology and to dispense medicines. The photograph shows a researcher preparing some droplets.

21. Gadgets and innovations

Philips has set itself the goal of improving the quality of life of three billion people by 2025. Quality of life is about more than just good health: people also need to be able to enjoy life, if possible by using Philips products. This is why Philips Research also conducts research into consumer lifestyle. Increased well-being, a growing demand for technologically advanced care products, the call for sustainable solutions and the increasing importance of design: by combining innovative technology and a deep understanding of what the customer wants, Philips aims to stand out from the crowd.

As a result of this, the research currently being conducted by Philips Research also has a softer side. It not only focuses on how a lamp is put together, for example, but also the effect that the radiated light has on the consumer's mood. Everything from Senseo coffee for breakfast to ambient television on the sofa in the evening: Philips is eager to find out how we feel in these situations. At the High Tech Campus, there is a HomeLab with its own control centre to monitor the experiences of the test subjects from all angles. There is also a Personal Care Institute that records precisely how we use an electric toothbrush, where researchers try out the latest hair-removal techniques on consumers and where ultrasound is used to combat ageing of the skin.

In our living environment, Ambient Intelligence has become an unstoppable phenomenon. The home of the near future will be equipped with a network of intelligent systems that provide us with information, entertain us or lighten our mood. Examples include a front door that recognises the occupant and opens automatically, the refrigerator that monitors if there is sufficient chilled beer available or clothing that informs the wearer when it needs to be washed. All of these systems communicate with us and with each other, respond effectively to changes in circumstances and think ahead. They are also so small that they can easily be concealed.

Experiment on the experience of sound in a dead room (anechoic chamber), where the walls absorb the sound.

Interactive museum

Visitors to this museum are not issued with a standard floor plan but are directed around it by light integrated within the interactive flooring. The work of art that one visitor creates in real-time simultaneously appears in the digital catalogue of his or her fellow visitor. The boy in front of the Night Watch does not even have a catalogue. He is downloading information about Rembrandt using the artwork itself.

Personalised bus shelter

This boy is using his smartphone to give the bus shelter his own personal touch.

Paying by telephone

With a mobile telephone equipped with Near Field Communication, you can pay for your ticket simply by holding your phone close to the terminal.

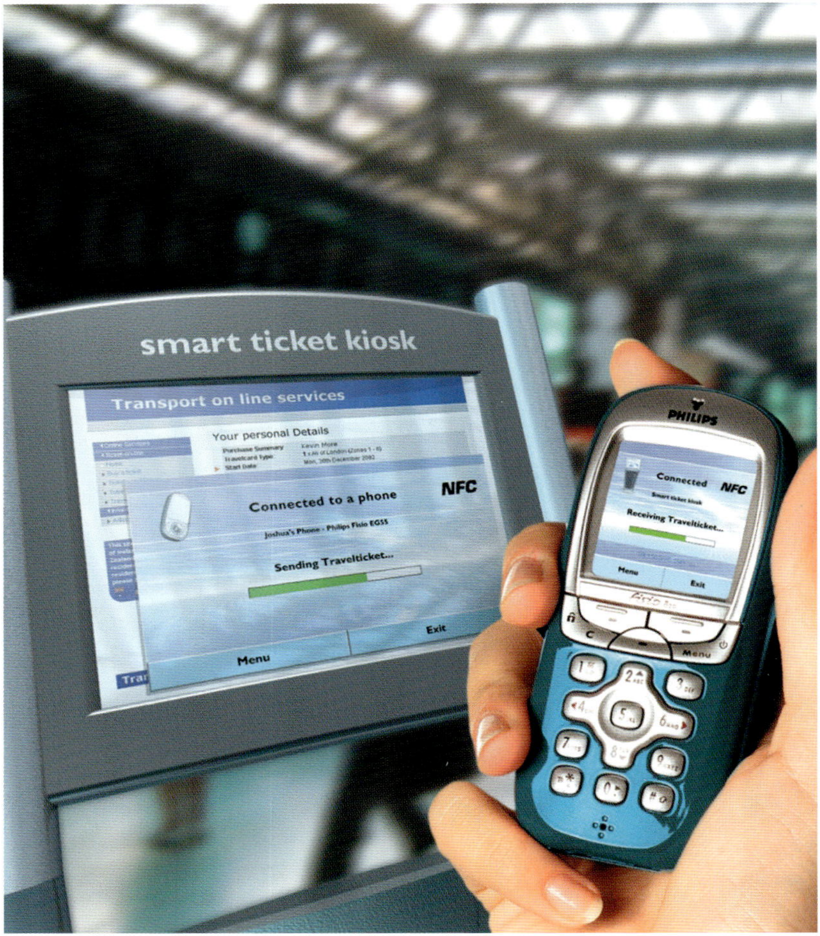

3D-gaming

Psychological and physiological measurements of the experiences of a test subject deeply involved in a 3D game.

The helpful cat

iCat is a prototype of a user-friendly personal robot that can provide help with everyday chores.

ExperienceLab

The Philips ExperienceLab offers unique opportunities for multidisciplinary research. Teams of psychologists, sociologists and designers can observe the reactions of test subjects using new technology.

The perfect curl

A researcher at the Personal Care Institute inspects the results of a hairstyling experiment.

Cook like a chef

The Jamie Oliver HomeCooker stirs, sets the right temperature and monitors the cooking time all by itself. Melting, simmering, boiling, steaming, braising – the HomeCooker does it all, at least according to the advertising. The appliance can also turn its hand to home-made soup, fried potatoes, risotto and paella. There is no accounting for tastes. But please note: those in the know advise against using the HomeCooker for steak.

e-Skin

'E-skin' technology enables a smart phone or MP3 player to turn any colour you wish. At the touch of a button, its appearance changes to match your clothes or mood.

Ultra low power

For electronic applications on or in the human body, for example wireless sensors that detect and send signals, being able to operate at very low power is essential. The picture shows a circuit board for a so-called DC/DC converter. This piece of miniature electronics converts the voltage of a direct current power source to a different value.

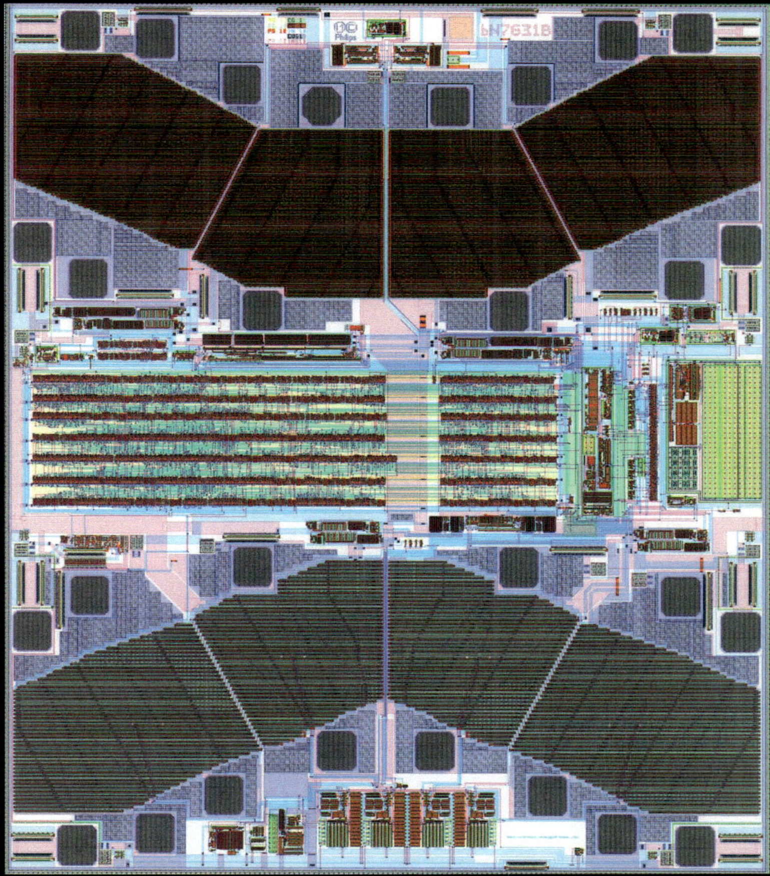

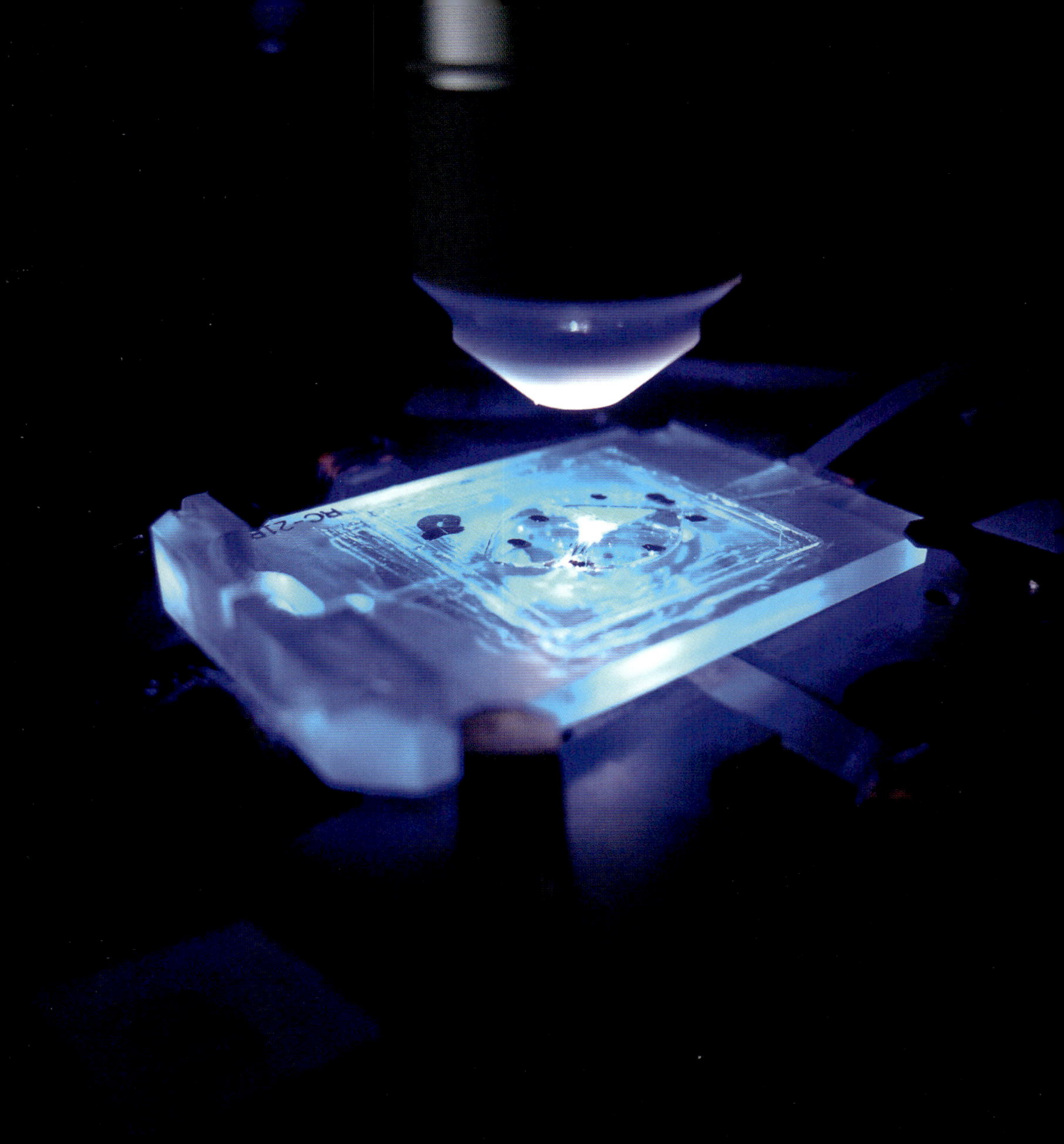

22. Open Innovation

There is a remarkable photo from 2003 showing the claw of a bulldozer that has just grasped a metres-wide sign saying PHILIPS RESEARCH, ripped the monster from the ground and is about to continue its demolition work. The sign marked the site in Waalre where Philips had its Physics Laboratory in the 1960s. Originally, it was an hermetically-sealed site with barriers and a porter at the gate. All that changed in 1998, when Philips Research concentrated all of its Dutch research facilities in Waalre, removed the barrier and created an open campus. In 2003, Philips opened up the site as a base for other innovative companies and the High Tech Campus Eindhoven became a reality – the Philips Research sign was now surplus to requirements.

The campus now accommodates more than 100 companies and institutes and around 8,000 researchers, entrepreneurs and other knowledge workers are active there.
The guiding principle is open innovation, which means that Philips and the other HTC residents share facilities and exchange knowledge. This open innovation was given a boost in 2000 when a group of semiconductor researchers from Philips Research relocated to IMEC in Leuven to make use of the clean room facilities of this leading international centre for microelectronics. Suddenly, the clean room (a dust-free room used to manufacture chips, for example) on the campus in Eindhoven was half-empty and the question arose as to whether it could be of some use to IMEC. That proved to be the case. In 2005, the Holst Centre came into being at the initiative of Philips Research, an alliance between IMEC and the Netherlands Organisation for Applied Scientific Research (TNO) focusing on the development of innovative technologies for autonomous wireless sensors and flexible electronics.

Philips also looks beyond Eindhoven for its partners and contacts with the academic world date back as far as the establishment of the NatLab. Gilles Holst was a professor by special appointment in Leiden and there were many who came after him. Research collaborates with hundreds of universities and other knowledge institutions and 25 of its staff work as part-time professors in the Netherlands and abroad. Open innovation is all about give and take.

Magnetic biosensor made by the research group of Philips Fellow Menno Prins.

The Holst Centre

The Holst Centre was established in 2005 with the support of the Dutch Ministry of Economic Affairs and the government of Flanders. It takes its name from Gilles Holst, the first director of the Philips NatLab. Based at the High Tech Campus Eindhoven, the Holst Centre benefits from the state-of-the-art facilities on site. The Holst Centre has more than 160 employees of 28 nationalities and more than 30 industrial partners.

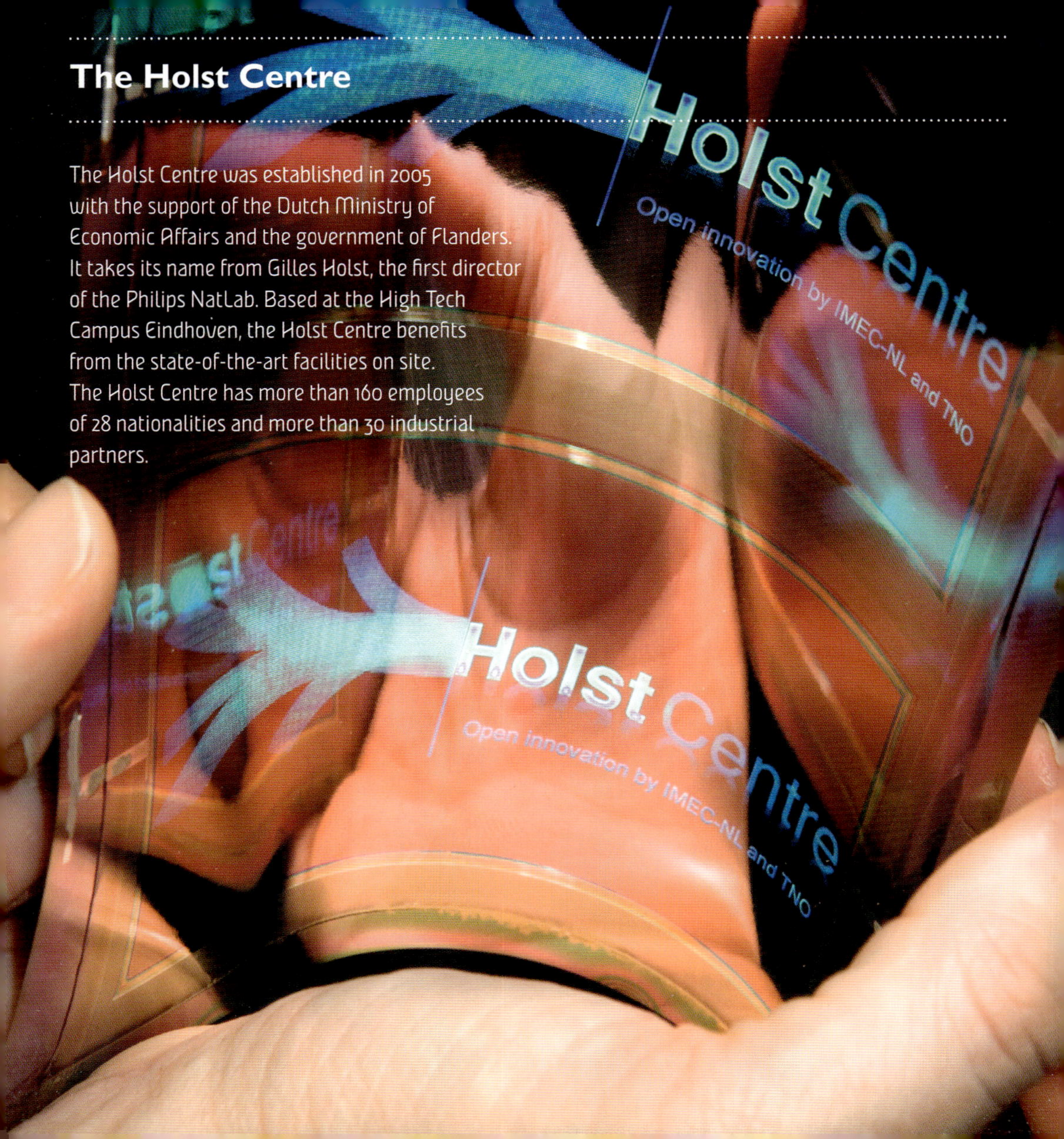

EIRMA

EIRMA is the European Industrial Research Management Association. Partly at the initiative of Hendrik Casimir, the organisation was established in 1966 and now includes around 120 European companies, ranging from engineering consultancy ABB to Volvo. It operates as a platform for companies with Research & Development departments, focusing in particular on management aspects.

Digital pathology system

The Erasmus Medical Centre in Rotterdam and Philips are working together on the digital analysis of cells and tissues. This will enable faster diagnosis and the quality of diagnoses will also be enhanced by the high resolution of the tissue imaging. Analyses of small tissue samples was a laborious process until now. Sending the samples takes time and involves risk of damage. The digital pathology system, developed by Philips, a combination of rapid scans and software to process and analyse the images, means that pathologists no longer need to stare into a microscope.

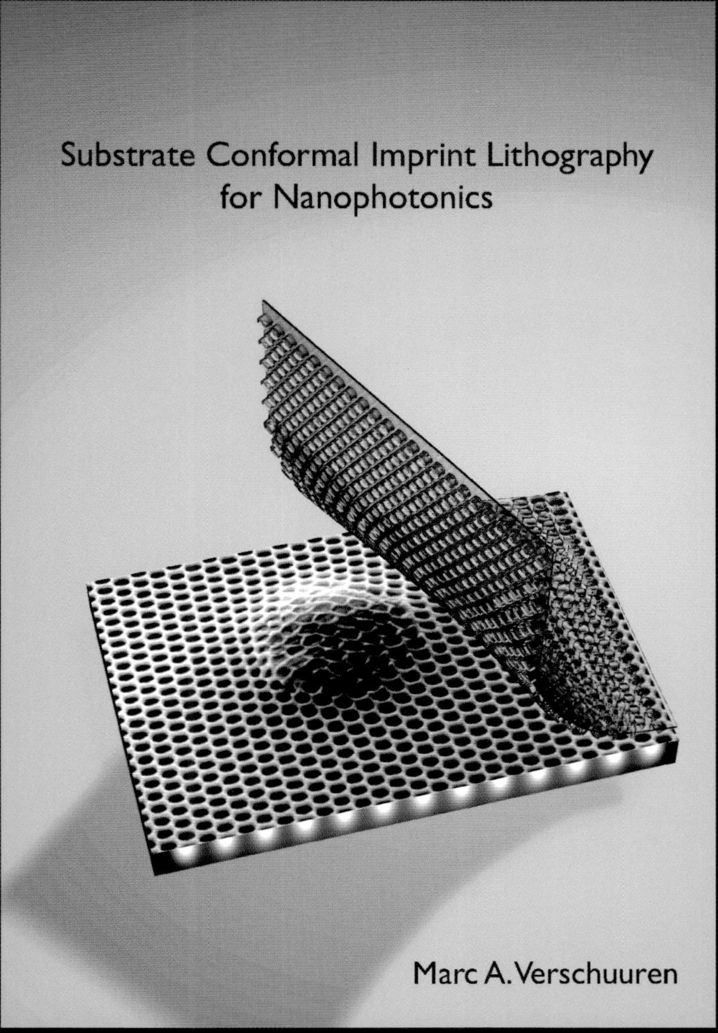

Nanophotonics

AMOLF, a physics research institute run by the FOM Foundation for Fundamental Research on Matter, has a world-famous Nanophotonics Centre. Part of its research, the interaction between light and the surface of nanostructures is being conducted at the High Tech Campus in Eindhoven, enabling close collaboration with Philips Research. Ultimately, the research will deliver applications relating to more efficient solar cells, optical sensors and new light sources. The picture shows an anti-reflective coating developed by AMOLF and Philips that significantly enhances the performance of solar cells.

Research fellow Menno Prins

Menno Prins is one of the many people who combine a position at Philips Research with an appointment as a part-time professor at a university. Prins, who came to Eindhoven in 1995 and was awarded his PhD on an experimental physics subject in Nijmegen is conducting research at Philips Research into biosensors in the context of the 'lab on a chip' – the functions of a laboratory

integrated on a chip, including microfluidics. At Eindhoven University of Technology, Prins also heads up a group researching the same subject. The magnetic biosensors are made with conventional chip manufacturing techniques, after which they are printed with proteins using the inkjet printer method.

Dutch physicists

In 1921, the physics journal *Physica* was founded by Balthasar van der Pol and Ekko Oosterhuis, both of whom were associated with the NatLab. Philips Research continues to play an important role in the world of physics. For example, Henk van Houten, director of Philips Research, sits on the board of the FOM, the organisation that funds physics research in the Netherlands. Van Houten joined Philips in 1985 and conducted pioneering quantum research in Eindhoven with Carlo Beenakker (who returned to the university in 1992 after operation Centurion). On 8 April 2011, Henk van Houten presented the University of Leiden with a plaque on behalf of Philips Research commemorating the role of Gilles Holst to mark the celebration of 100 years of superconductivity.

High-precision irradiation

The integration of MRI scanners with radiotherapy is a new development, enabling radiation to be used to combat tumours from outside the body. Because the brain can be viewed throughout the process, the radiologist can directly see the impact that the treatment is having. Philips developed such a combined system with Utrecht University Medical Centre, with the Utrecht professor of clinical physics initiating the project and initial government support coming from the Technology Foundation STW.

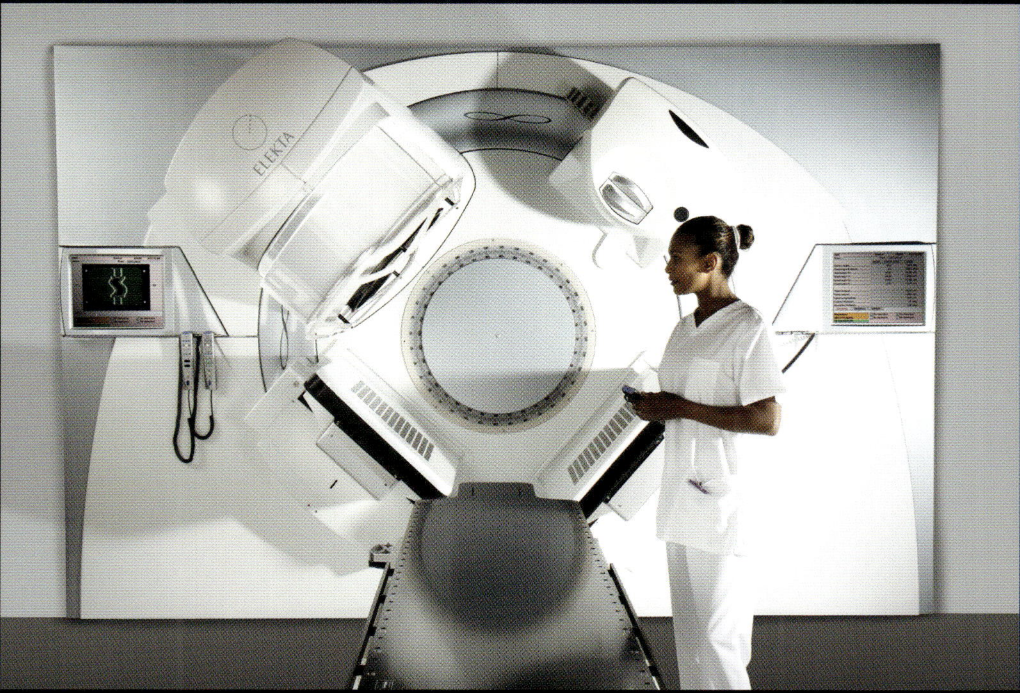

MiPlaza

MiPlaza is part of Philips Innovation Services and the High Tech Campus Eindhoven. Philips Innovation Services forms the backbone of the HTC infrastructure. It provides 20,000 m² of multifunctional laboratories, including clean rooms, test labs, a variety of electrical engineering facilities, 15,000 instruments and a special room for pilot manufacturing. Philips Innovation Services has around 500 clients, ranging from start-ups to multinationals.

Young people and technology

Philips contributes to JetNet, established in 2003 to bring secondary school students into contact with industrial laboratories. JetNet is the Dutch acronym for Youth and Technology Network in the Netherlands and is an alliance between government, industry and education. The aim is to spark an interest in technology among young people by means of masterclasses, workshops, internships, expert supervision and special guided tours. One of the activities is the Girls Day, which aims to interest girls in secondary schools in a career in research and technology.

23. Visions of the future

How does Philips envisage tomorrow's world? At the Philips Innovation Experience held in November 2012 in the Klokgebouw, once a Philips factory and now the beating heart of creative Eindhoven, CEO Frans van Houten (the brother of Henk van Houten, director of Philips Research) presented his vision. He sees three Grand Challenges that he aims to take on:

'One: between now and 2050, the world population will increase from seven to nine billion people. Over two-thirds of these people will live in towns and cities, and that figure will be around 80% in Europe. Improving the quality of life in cities, making them smarter, safer, and more sustainable and providing for sufficient food and drinking water is an enormous challenge.'

'Two: in the developed countries, the population is ageing rapidly. The good news is that, in the future, most of us will live longer. Currently, 900 million people in the world are over the age of sixty. By 2050, that figure is expected to have increased to 2.4 billion. The not so good news is that, by 2050, 50% of the world's population will be suffering from some form of chronic disease, such as diabetes or cancer. This will lead to a significant increase in the demand for high-quality, accessible healthcare. This will cost money and human effort: will there be enough to go around?'

'Three: the massive increase in the population will result in a growing demand for energy, food and water. If we fail to act on the supply side, worldwide energy consumption is expected to increase by 50% in the next twenty years, and the same will happen to the demand for food. At the same time, millions of people will suffer from a shortage of drinking water, partly as a result of climate change.'

For this reason, Philips' mission is to make a substantial contribution to help solve these Grand Challenges. 'Our aim is, by 2025, to improve the lives of three billion people every year by developing useful and innovative solutions, thereby contributing to a healthier and more sustainable world.'

Cheaper crops

Philips Lighting is conducting research into the effects of LED lighting on the growth of a variety of different crops. It is supplying 'light recipes' that provide an indication of the necessary light intensity, the colours that the light spectrum should include, where the lights should be positioned and when they should be activated. The result of this 'City Farming' is that the crops grow better and costs are reduced.

Acoustic ceiling

The office of the future will have a Soundlight Comfort Ceiling. It is an acoustic ceiling with integrated LED lighting. Evenly-lit surfaces across the entire ceiling or islands of light are used to create calm and a natural feeling of space. If you also add to that the sound absorption, which makes nearby sounds easier to hear and more distant sounds less easy, the concentration of employees is improved massively, as is the intention.

Intelligent shop window

In its ShopLab, Philips Research is working on intelligent shop windows. They provide potential customers with the opportunity to request information about the products displayed in the shop window, even when the shop has closed.

Incision-free surgery

MR-HIFU is a technology that offers an alternative to surgical intervention. HIFU stands for High-Intensity Focused Ultrasound. By combining imaging via an MRI scanner with ultrasound treatment, tumour cells can be precisely targeted. This virtually pain-free treatment method has already been used to remove uterine fibroids.

In the University Medical Center in Utrecht, research is being conducted on the extent to which the technology can be used to combat breast cancer. The MR-HIFU scanner can also track drugs used to combat cancer in the body in order to check that they have reached their target.

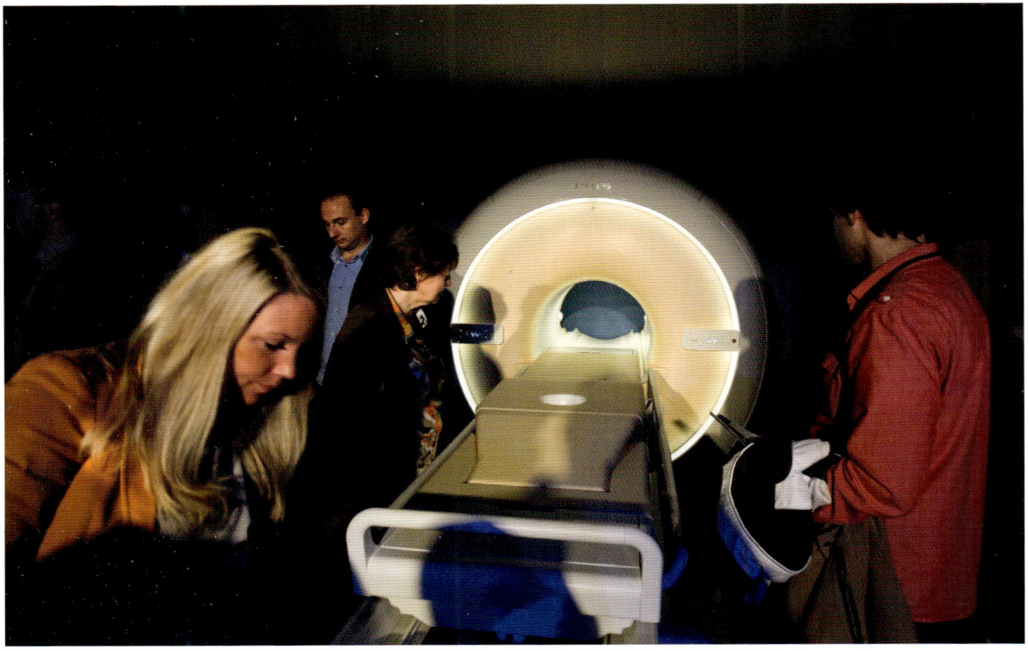

Lighting provides the right information at the right time

Philips is developing intelligent lighting for professional applications that enable information to be transmitted. The technology makes it possible for lighting to display information to a visitor or customer on their smartphone or tablet at exactly the right time. It has potential for use in museums. As soon as the visitor is within range of the 'intelligent light', he or she receives information that is relevant to a specific artwork. Or the 'intelligent light' can guide the visitor through the most interesting route in the museum. Intelligent lighting also has potential for use in supermarkets, shopping centres and airports.

Flexible electronics

Various electronic components and test circuits have been printed on this flexible foil made from polyamide (nylon). Bending or folding the foil has no effect on the functioning of the circuits.

Sustainable wood-burning stove

Philips aims to improve the quality of life of billions of people. For example, in developing countries through the use of the wood-burning stove developed by Philips Research. An electronically-controlled ventilator blows air through the stove, increasing its performance and greatly reducing smoke emissions. The ventilator is powered by a thermoelectric generator combined with the heat of the burning wood.

NanoLED

Nanothreads, a thousand times thinner than a human hair, are ideal for nanoLEDs. Philips has developed these structures in alliance with researchers from the Kavli Institute for Nanosciences at Delft University of Technology. They have potential for use in opto-electronics: electronics that respond to light. Ultimately, Philips hopes to be able to use the technology to make white LED lighting.

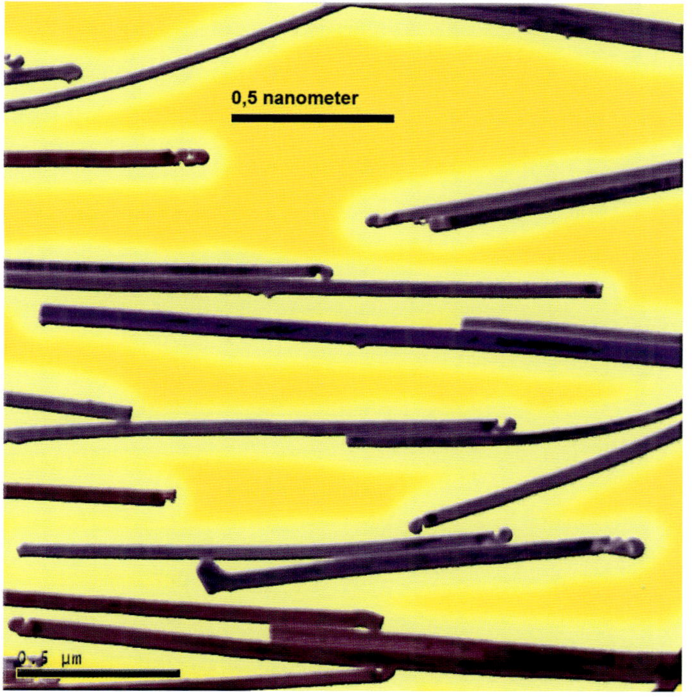

Radio Frequency Identification

Philips Research is developing RFID tags (radio frequency identification) based on plastic electronics, for tracking and monitoring objects or living beings. The tags are as thin as newsprint and the size of a postage stamp.

Bibliography

- Blanken, I.J., *De ontwikkeling van de N.V. Philips' gloeilampenfabriek tot elektrotechnisch concern* [Geschiedenis van Philips Electronics N.V. Deel III (1922-1934)] (Leiden 1992)
- Blanken, I.J. , *Onder Duits beheer* [Geschiedenis van Philips Electronics N.V. Deel IV] (Zaltbommel 1997)
- Blanken, I.J. *Een industriële wereldfederatie* [Geschiedenis van Koninklijke Philips Electronics N.V. Deel V] (Zaltbommel 2002)
- Boersma, K., 'De ontwikkeling van röntgentechnologie in de beginjaren van het Philips' Natuurkundig Laboratorium', in *NEHA-Jaarboek 1999*, pp. 291-318.
- Boersma, K., *Inventing structures for industrial research: a history of the Philips NatLab 1914-1946* (Amsterdam 2002)
- Casimir, H.B.G., *Het toeval van de werkelijkheid: een halve eeuw natuurkunde* (Meulenhoff 1983)
- Derks, S., *Philishave: generations of shaving excellence* (Eindhoven, Groningen 1998)
- Elsken, Ed van der, *NATLAB* (Eindhoven 1989)
- Heerding, A., *Het ontstaan van de Nederlandse gloeilampenindustrie* [Geschiedenis van de N.V. Philips' gloeilampenfabriek. Deel 1] ('s-Gravenhage 1980)
- Heerding, A., *Een onderneming van vele markten thuis* [Geschiedenis van N.V. Philips' gloeilampenfabriek. Deel 2] (Leiden 1986)
- Hutter, J.J., *Toepassingsgericht onderzoek in de industrie: de ontwikkeling van kwikdamplampen* (Helmond 1988)
- Maas, A., 'Van verstild lichtspel tot opdringerig beeldborbardement', *Nederlands tijdschrift voor natuurkunde*, 76 (2010) pp. 284-286.
- Marzano, Stefan (ed.), *Past tense future sense : competing through creativity: 80 years of design at Philips* (BIS Publishers 2005)
- Metze, M., *Kortsluiting: hoe Philips zijn talenten verspilde* (Nijmegen 1991)
- Metze, M., *Let's make things better* (Nijmegen 1997)
- Peek, H.B., 'The emergence of the compact disc', *IEEE communications magazine, January* 2010, pp. 10-17
- *Popular electronics: early Dutch electronic music from Philips Research Laboratories, 1956-1963* [CD box with documentation, complied by K. Tazelaar and D. Raaijmakers (Basta Music 2004)]

- Schoenher, S., 'The history of magnetic recording' [presented at the IEEE Magnetics Society Seminar, UCSD, 2 November 2002]
- Vles, H., *Hallo Bandoeng: Nederlandse radiopioniers [1900-1945]* (Zutphen 2008)
- Vries, M.J. de, *80 years of research at the Philips Natuurkundig Laboratorium 1914-1994* [with contributions by F. Kees Boersma] (Amsterdam 2005)
- We also consulted the following excellent Wikipedia pages: ' Fluorescentielamp'; 'Gramophone record' and 'Geluidsdragers door de tijd'.

Illustrations

With the exception of the following list, all illustrations used in this book have been sourced from the Philips Company Archives.

- Museum Boerhaave, Leiden: 28, 46, 56, 60, 61, 63, 83, 102 (right), 106, 145, 146, 148, 286, 287
- Philips Research, Eindhoven (photography Marloes Bogaarts): 33, 94
- Stichting tot Behoud van Historische Philips Producten, Eindhoven (photography Marloes Bogaarts): 192
- H. Peek, Nuenen (photography Marloes Bogaarts): 162
- Het Radio Amateur Museum, Reusel: 67
- Museum voor Communicatie, Den Haag: 134, 135
- Archief Centrum Wiskunde & Informatica, Amsterdam: 194
- NXP, Nijmegen: 197
- TU Eindhoven: 260, 266
- EIRMA, Brussel: 263
- AMOLF, Amsterdam: 265
- Leiden Institute of Physics: 268
- TU Delft: 281
- Nobel Foundation, Stockholm: 47
- Connected Cambridge: 209

About the authors

Dirk van Delft is Director of Museum Boerhaave and professor by special appointment in Material Heritage of Natural Science at the University of Leiden. He was previously chief science editor for the newspaper *NRC Handelsblad*. His research focuses on physics in the Netherlands in the period after 1880, the start of the 'Second Golden Age'. Van Delft's publications include works on Heike Kamerlingh Onnes, Ehrenfest and Einstein in Leiden. In 2005, he was awarded the NWO Eureka Prize for science communication. His PhD thesis, a biography of Dutch physicist Heike Kamerlingh Onnes (published by Bert Bakker), was on the AKO literature prize long-list in the same year.

Ad Maas is curator at Museum Boerhaave. As such, he has been responsible for various exhibitions including 'Einstein in the Netherlands' and '100 YEARS OF INVENTIONS; made by Philips Research'. Maas was awarded his PhD in 2001 for his thesis on physics in Amsterdam entitled *Atomisme en Individualisme. De Amsterdamse natuurkunde tussen 1877 en 1940* (Verloren, Hilversum). The focus of his research is primarily modern science. He has published widely on the history of science.

Museum Boerhave

Museum Boerhaave is the Dutch National Museum for the history of science and medicine, based in the centre of Leiden. Its mission is to use its unique collection that spans five centuries of innovation in the Netherlands to appeal to, captivate, educate and entertain a large and wide-ranging public – whilst never losing sight of current issues in society. Museum Boerhaave considers science to be an essential part of Dutch culture.

Its collection includes some milestones from the history of Dutch science: microscopes by Antoni van Leeuwenhoek, who was visited by Tsar Peter the Great to try the microscope out for himself, the renowned pendulum clocks developed by Christiaan Huygens, the Netherlands' greatest ever genius, and the installations used by Heike Kamerlingh Onnes in 1908 to create the 'coldest place on Earth'. It also features major medical inventions, including Willem Einthoven's very first ECG machine and the artificial lung that Willem Kolff had made in the Second World War.

Museum Boerhaave exhibits these objects as a cohesive whole, set against the backdrop of the wider history. This gives them greater meaning and broadens public access.

Colophon

Philips Research. 100 years of inventions that matter, published to mark the exhibition '100 YEARS OF INVENTIONS, Made by Philips Research' in Museum Boerhaave, from 19 December 2013 to 26 October 2014.

Published by
WBOOKS, Zwolle
info@wbooks.com
www.wbooks.com
in alliance with
Museum Boerhaave, Leiden
informatie@museumboerhaave.nl
www.museumboerhaave.nl

Text
Dirk van Delft
Ad Maas

Design
Richard Bos, Wergea

Translation
UvA Talen, Amsterdam

ISBN 978 90 663 0458 1 (English)
ISBN 978 90 663 0571 7 (Dutch)
NUR 680
Third edition, 2014

W BOOKS

MUSEUM BOERHAAVE LEIDEN